PUNC

FOR

FICTION WRITERS

by

Rick Taubold, PhD & Scott Gamboe

ISBN-13: 9781512024081

ISBN-10: 1512024082

DEDICATION

To writers everywhere:

May you all be successful and see your dreams fulfilled.

NOTE TO READERS:

A detailed index for this book, referenced by section numbers, will be available as a free download from the authors' websites.

CONTENTS

INTRODUCTORY NOTES

[Intro.1] Reference dictionaries & style guides

In the US, the Merriam-Webster (M-W) unabridged dictionary is the generally accepted authority for spelling and word usage.

In the UK and in other countries using British English, the Oxford English Dictionary (OED) is the accepted authority. The OED exists in both UK and US versions. The OED US and M-W will usually agree, but here is one of our favorites:

> M-W: sweat shirt
> OED US: sweatshirt
> OED UK: sweat-shirt

More interesting is that most other current dictionaries show "sweatshirt." When such discrepancies occur, you may either go with the majority or follow the standard reference.

In another example, M-W shows "lightbulb" as one word, but most other dictionaries have it as two. The OED US shows the one-word form as an alternative.

Our standard reference style guide for this book is the Chicago Manual of Style (CMOS), the 16th edition as of this writing. Where the CMOS is silent or incomplete, we have researched the subject to provide you with the most authoritative answers and best practices.

The CMOS is the standard in much of the US book publishing industry, while the Associated Press (AP) Style Guide is often preferred for journalistic writing.

[Intro.2] Notes on the text & format of this book

[Intro.2.1] Displaying optional and incorrect commas

In some of our examples, we put a comma in parentheses (,) to denote it as optional, meaning one that the grammar rules say should be added but which may be omitted depending on one's punctuation style.

A comma in square brackets [,] denotes an incorrect comma, as we show in chapter 3 [3.3].

[Intro.2.2] Examples

We indent our examples and some of our tips and explanations to make them more visible. Multi-paragraph examples are also first-line indented.

[Intro.3] Computer key codes & settings

[Intro.3.1] ALT codes

Throughout this book we will mention how to insert certain pieces of punctuation that don't appear directly on your keyboard. One consistent method is to use ALT key codes on a Windows PC. You hold the ALT key while you type a 4-digit number on the *numeric* keypad.

For example, ALT 0033 inserts an exclamation mark (!), and ALT 0147 inserts a left smart quote ("). Although we intend for these to be used in MS Word, these codes will work in many other programs on the PC. In some cases, special keyboard shortcuts exist for symbols (e.g., é, à, ü) and special punctuation marks not on the keyboard. We've included some of the important ones.

A Mac computer does not use these same codes and employs a different system to enter special characters. We've included some of those.

[Intro.3.2] MS Word automatic replacement settings

MS Word has options for automatically converting certain key combinations into other things. Examples are changing a double hyphen (--) into an em-dash (—) and inserting smart quotes (" or ") instead of straight quotes ("). These are controlled in MS Word's Options. Check your particular version of MS Word for where to find them. In the "AutoCorrect Options" locate "AutoFormat as you type." Under the "Replace as you type" check or uncheck your choices.

CHAPTER ONE

WHY THIS BOOK?

The purpose of writing is to convey ideas. Punctuation in essence gives directions to the reader that help to convey those ideas and to control the flow of the writing. Further, it can add dimension by bringing the intonations and mannerisms of the characters' speech to the written word.

[1.1] What is punctuation?

Merriam Webster's Unabridged Dictionary defines punctuation as, "*The act, practice, or system of inserting various standardized marks or signs in written or printed matter in order to clarify the meaning and separate structural units.*"

Other references word it differently, but the key point in all of them is that punctuation serves to clarify meaning and to aid understanding. Our primary reason for writing this book is to teach you how to use punctuation to make your writing clearer and stronger.

[1.2] Why another book on punctuation?

A bazillion books and reference articles (and maybe a few stone tablets and papyrus scrolls) deal with punctuation. What's missing, in our opinion, is a punctuation book geared specifically to fiction writers, who need flexibility in order to convey the right voice in their writing. Some books suggest this flexibility, but few stress it.

Unlike many grammar and punctuation books, we approached this subject as fiction writers, not from a formal writing perspective. Rigid rules of punctuation and grammar are fine for formal writing. In textbooks, papers, newspapers, and magazine articles we want clean writing in a neutral voice. Journalists and academics accustomed to formal writing may struggle initially with writing fiction because they're used to keeping personalities and emotions out of the mix. Sometimes you have to bend rules in order to add those things to fiction.

We sought to create a compact, definitive, up-to-date reference with a broad range of relevant examples to meet the needs of both novice and experienced fiction writers, all without getting bogged down in hard rules, irrelevant details, and esoteric usage.

One of the best small books on punctuation that we've found is *Punctuate it Right!* by Harry Shaw, written in 1963. Although not specific to fiction, Shaw's excellent book met most of our criteria. Having been written in 1963, however, some parts of it are out of date. The state abbreviations had not been standardized with two letters and no periods, and some states were never abbreviated (N.Y., Md., Ala., Tenn., Iowa). Academic degrees were written with periods (B.A. and Ph.D.). Shaw's book (still available) is also missing some topics we feel are relevant to today's writing.

We do love one point that Shaw makes: "Punctuation is no longer a set of wholly absurd and arbitrary rules found only in style books and handbooks for writers and editors." That's even truer today than it was in 1963.

The Chicago Manual of Style (CMOS) is considered the definitive authority by most publishing houses in the US today. It's nearly exhaustive in its treatment of punctuation and is updated every few years. But aside from being around 1000 pages, it's a style book (not specifically a grammar book) designed for editors and publishers. Nevertheless, we advise every serious writer to consider purchasing it or subscribing to the online version for the wealth of valuable information it contains.

In addition to punctuation, our book includes a good dose of grammar and real-world applications. Chapter two contains the definitions, with examples, that we use. Each chapter begins with the basics and most chapters have an *Advanced* section to show you the finer points.

We based our book on American English punctuation. In the UK and in countries that follow UK style, some differences exist. We will point those out along the way, but most of what we present here applies no matter which style of English you're using.

> NOTE: Different style guides take different approaches to punctuation (comma-rich vs. comma-sparse, for example), and some publishing houses deviate from the CMOS.

[1.3] Tools, not rules

Many people view punctuation as a set of rules, but this is incorrect thinking. Rules tell you what you should or should not do. Punctuation marks represent a set of conventions, not pronouncements. Grammar teachers don't tell you that the "rules" of grammar are really conventions of use, not laws of writing decided by some legislative body whose dictates we must follow or suffer some penalty for breaking.

We prefer to view punctuation marks as a set of tools to help writers express themselves. Rules rarely help you find the *best* way to punctuate in a given situation. Tools, in contrast, help you craft and shape your work. While we will still refer to "rules" (because it's a short and succinct word), we really mean conventions.

Punctuation is not about following rules but about making the writing easier to read. We will therefore sometimes advocate going against the established conventions. Humans don't always think or speak in complete, grammatically correct sentences. Why should the characters we write about be any different? Consider the following sentences:

She entered the room and stopped.

She entered the room, and stopped.

She entered the room. And stopped.

According to the current, formal rules, only the first one is correctly punctuated. In the second, the comma is considered unnecessary, and in the third, the second sentence is a fragment, something grammar teachers tell us we should *never* write. Yet each of these examples conveys a different shade of meaning. Must we ignore two of those meanings simply because the "rules" forbid us?

We're not saying that the rules do not matter. Formal grammar has its place, and every writer should learn and understand it. We will show you the formal rules, then we'll show you when it's acceptable to break them for more expressive writing.

Consider a more complicated example below. Each variation conveys a different mood, and not all of them follow the formal rules.

Often in the middle of the night I wake up screaming.

Often in the middle of the night I wake up, screaming.

Often in the middle of the night, I wake up screaming.

Often, in the middle of the night, I wake up screaming.

Often, in the middle of the night, I wake up: screaming.

Often, in the middle of the night, I wake up. Screaming.

Languages evolve and change through our need to communicate. One has only to look at the language in Shakespeare's plays to see that. Likewise, grammar is not a set of rules but a description of language usage.

For example, students have struggled whether to use *who* or *whom* in a given situation, but *whom* has now mostly dropped out of all but formal situations, displaced in both our speech and writing in the same way that *thee* and *thou* fell out of use.

[1.4] The origins of punctuation

Many people believe that punctuation is part of the grammar of the language, but the two are separate. Grammar explains how the language is structured, while punctuation serves to separate the grammatical elements in sentences. The *primary* purpose of punctuation is to clarify the meaning of the writing. In other words, punctuation exists for the *reader's* benefit.

Some references attribute the rise of punctuation to the development of the printing press. The rise of printing in the 14th and 15th centuries certainly contributed to the need for punctuation standards, but examples of punctuation can be found as far back as Greek writing in the 5th century BC and in some Ancient Egyptian writing. Most sources agree that it arose from the need to clarify in the written language those things that would otherwise be apparent in the spoken language: pauses, emphasis, and intonation.

The need for punctuation was recognized by groups of Hebrew scribe-scholars known as the Masoretes, who worked mainly between the 5th and 10th centuries AD to preserve the Biblical texts. At that time, the Hebrew language had no written vowels. They existed only in the spoken language. Concerned that the pronunciation of the sacred texts would become corrupted or lost, the Masoretes devised a set of vowel markings—still in use today in modern Hebrew—along with a set of accent marks that told the speaker precisely how the text should be read aloud (or chanted in this case). They were stage directions of a sort.

While the Masoretic punctuation system bears no resemblance to our present English one, its existence demonstrates that the limitations of a written language based solely on words were recognized centuries ago. In a time before recording devices capable of capturing the nuances of the spoken word existed, the Masoretes achieved it in their system of writing. Hebrew was not the only early language lacking written vowels. The earliest alphabetic writing also lacked capital letters and spaces, which didn't matter because writing at the time was used primarily for business transactions. The Roman alphabet was originally all capital letters, and lowercase came later.

Early punctuation in English was also aimed at the spoken word instead of the written one. George Bernard Shaw said that punctuation was an aid to reading aloud, and as late as the end of the 18th century, punctuation was still treated this way.

English punctuation came into existence with the printing press, but the use of the various marks didn't always make sense. In the late 1400s, the period represented both a pause as well as the end of a sentence. A couple of centuries later, writers attempted to establish rigid rules for the comma, semicolon, and colon. The comma represented a brief pause, the semicolon was twice as long a pause as a comma, and a colon was twice as long a pause as the semicolon.

By the end of the 19th century, punctuation began to be used more to show the grammatical divisions and connections among the parts of a sentence instead of how the sentence should be read aloud. Thus, the period came to mean not a pause after a thought but the end of the grammatical unit of the sentence, which was also grammatically defined. This is when many of our current "rules" came into existence.

[1.5] The necessity of punctuation

Punctuation interrupts the prose. Like traffic signals and signs designed to control drivers, punctuation controls the narrative. The

12

rules of punctuation exist for common understanding. Changing them arbitrarily is comparable to changing the colors and positions of the lights in traffic signals or the shape of the standard stop sign. Our writer friend Perry Mc Daid offered the following advice and example:

Some quarters today seem to think that punctuation is optional or even unnecessary, as we see in e-mail and text messages. While we tolerate those situations, we must realize that (especially in the cyber-world) we live in a multicultural society where accents, culture, and personal viewpoints can misconstrue the meanings of sentences. Punctuation is as critical to communication as the actual wording. Literature is all about communication.

Take, for example, the vernacular expression of an unbridled celebration of food: Go on pig out.

> Go on pig-out. (With a hyphen we have a reminder of an upcoming event.)

> Go on, pig out! (Now we have an instruction or command to help yourself at a meal.)

> Go on, pig, out! (We can have it be an insult and a command to leave.)

> Go... on pig... out. (We're chasing out someone who has galloped into the house with an unusual steed.)

> Go! On pig. Out! (And we can give the previous version greater intensity.)

"This playful and simplistic example should convince you of the necessity of punctuation, for although a writer should always give readers the benefit of the doubt as regards intelligence, common sense is not universal in identity." (Perry Mc Daid)

[1.6] A practical approach to punctuation

Only twelve punctuation marks are common in fiction writing: period, question mark, exclamation mark, comma, semicolon, apostrophe, hyphen, colon, quotation mark, dash, ellipsis, parentheses.

Some would include brackets [ ], braces { }, and the forward slash (/) to make fifteen. These are rarely used in fiction, but we have included them in appropriate chapters.

Periods (plus question marks) and commas are the mainstays and the best marks for most purposes. Hyphens and apostrophes serve as spelling marks to alter or modify the meaning or grammatical purpose of certain words (the apostrophe to indicate possession, for example). Quotation marks serve mainly for setting off dialogue.

The other marks (including the exclamation mark) are largely decorative, accents as it were, and are rarely essential. Like any decorations, if they get out of hand, they can overshadow what they're supposed to be accenting. Imagine a Christmas tree so laden with lights and ornaments that the tree itself is no longer visible and serves merely as a framework for its decorations.

If you punctuate your writing as though it were being read aloud and employ good writing craft with it, you will make your writing strong and more precise and convey the subtleties of your prose.

Some editors will take a strict grammatical approach, putting punctuation marks where the "rules" say they belong. Along those lines, let's look at how two supposedly firm grammar rules originated. Why is it supposedly incorrect to end a sentence with a preposition and to split an infinitive? Why is the famous phrase from *Star Trek* "To boldly go where no man has gone before" instead of "to go boldly" an alleged grammar violation?

Back in the 17th and 18th centuries, a few influential men decided that English grammar ought to be more like that of Latin (ignoring the fact that English didn't originate from Latin in the first place). In Latin the infinitive verb form (to + verb: to go, to speak, to live) was a single entity and couldn't be split, so they reasoned that English should be no different.

In Latin, prepositions always came before the noun and therefore could not fall at the end of a sentence. Again, this was part of Latin grammar and had no place in English grammar. Even though the word "*pre*position" means that it must come before or *pre*cede the noun, writers back into the 1200s had long been ending sentences with prepositions. For decades, students have been taught these arbitrary pronouncements, and we still encounter people who honestly believe it's a grammatical sin to end a sentence with a preposition.

But we digress.

Because punctuation exists to make our writing intelligible to our readers, we're allowed some flexibility. While casual and less scholarly readers might not care much about our placement of commas, serious readers will. If you want your readers to take you and your work seriously, convince them that you know what you're doing. Sloppy grammar and punctuation will tell your readers that you don't care about your writing. So why should they?

If a reader has to stop unnecessarily or go back over something to make sense of it, then you haven't done your job. If this happens frequently, an annoyed reader may stop reading your book, not a desirable situation for you.

Your prerogative as a writer is to punctuate however best conveys your intent, but if you employ some bizarre technique without a clear purpose, you take a huge risk. Some writers who choose to write dialogue without quotation marks get away with it; other times they alienate readers. Cleverness has its limits.

In writing this book, we have researched what's out there and have sought to give you the best advice to cover as many situations as possible. Our book will make you aware of the current conventions and give you the confidence to stretch those conventions where needed.

You might ask why a writer can't make his or her life easy and simply follow the standard rules taught in school and in the grammar textbooks. The reason is that so many exceptions and options exist that the rules can become murky, and attempting to follow them strictly can lead to perfect—but sterile—prose.

Many times a comma will coincide with pause in speech if the line were read aloud. However, suggesting to someone from the Punctuation Police that a comma can be inserted anywhere you would pause in speech will likely get you cursed to a circle of Hell reserved for English grammar reprobates. The reasoning is valid: a pause in speech doesn't always mean a comma should be inserted in the written form. And we definitely do *not* advocate this practice.

In *Pinckert's Practical Grammar* (out of print), the author cites several alleged immutable punctuation rules: use a comma after a long introductory phrase; use a comma before a coordinating conjunction (e.g., and, but) that joins independent clauses; never use a period or semicolon before "and" or "but." Pinckert cites examples by famous speakers to prove his point that these rules are not immutable.

"My father taught me to work; he did not teach me to love it." (Abraham Lincoln)

"Better we lose the election than mislead the people; and better we lose than misgovern the people." (Adlai Stevenson)

"Give us the tools and we will finish the job." (Winston Churchill)

"My theory is to enjoy life. But my practice is against it." (Charles Lamb)

Are we to consider these learned individuals wrong for disobeying the rules? Although Lincoln's quote follows the rules, there is no rule that says a semicolon is better than a period. The last three quotes break the formal rules.

Some authors hold to the use of minimal punctuation or to such practices as not using quotation marks for direct dialogue. Notable among these are James Joyce (1882–1941) and Cormac McCarthy (1933–). Joyce condemned "inverted commas" (the British term for single quotation marks) and instead used a single dash to introduce a line of dialog. (See chapter 15 for examples.)

McCarthy has stated, "I believe in periods, in capitals, in the occasional comma, and that's it." He has cautioned that when you leave out such things as quotation marks, you have to write in such a way as not to confuse your readers. He has also said that if you write properly, you shouldn't have to punctuate.

We won't argue against a writer's choice to use minimal punctuation, but we will say that the ability to write clearly and unambiguously without punctuation requires considerable talent and effort on the part of the writer. If punctuation weren't necessary, it would likely not have come into existence. Further, the use of minimal punctuation may put an extra burden on the reader, who might not appreciate having to work to understand the writing.

Certainly, writers like Joyce and McCarthy have their critics. As with any writing conventions, you go against them at your own risk.

We can't stress enough that the guiding principle of any method of punctuation should be to use the right mark to convey your intent to the reader. The original purpose of punctuation was for elocution: to translate the written word into the spoken word. While printed matter is designed to be read, not spoken, the reader should still be able to hear your words in his head, and if he chooses to read them aloud, the sounds should be preserved in the writing.

Punctuation conventions provide a common framework for understanding. You can bend or break them only if you recognize that you're doing so and you ensure that your reader understands your intent.

We add one note here. Throughout this book we'll continue to stress the importance of punctuation to sentence meaning, but we also want to advise you that you should try to cast your sentences so that they aren't prey to punctuation. In other words, let punctuation enhance your writing, but avoid letting the meaning of your sentences depend solely on the punctuation.

Whatever style of punctuation you develop—minimal, liberal, strict, or creative—three guiding principles will help:

(1) The purpose of punctuation is to make your writing *clear* to your reader.

(2) Too little punctuation can confuse the same as too much.

(3) Punctuation should never call attention to itself. Anything unconventional or strange-looking may distract your reader and disturb the flow of the writing.

Even the best of us will struggle from time to time with figuring out whether a comma is correct in a given location or how to punctuate a particular sentence or passage. As you go through the rest of this book, we'll do our best to cover as many situations as possible.

Commas in particular are troublesome for many people. When in doubt about a comma, find the rule or convention that allows you to put a comma in that spot. If you can't find one—even if it sounds as if you need a comma—then don't use it. When your instinct tells you that you need some sort of pause or break, consider the other pieces of punctuation. Do not punctuate indiscriminately.

We hope that by the time you finish reading our book you will have developed a good instinct for where and when to use the various punctuation marks effectively.

Before we move on, we want to give you one important piece of advice. Throughout this book we will show how punctuation alone can change the meaning of a sentence, but you should *not* let punctuation be the sole decider. Never assume that every reader will appreciate the subtle difference between restrictive and nonrestrictive clauses, for example. Your job as a writer is to ensure that the reader completely understands your meaning.

> TIP: When the meaning could be misunderstood even with correct punctuation, reword the sentence to eliminate possible misreading.

CHAPTER TWO

GRAMMAR TERMS

To help you though this book, we've listed the grammar terms that we use along with examples.

[2.1] Phrases, clauses, and sentences

A *phrase* is a group of words that lacks a subject working with a verb:

> into the night, building a house, dressed in a tuxedo, with a guy

A *clause* is a group of words that does have a subject working with a finite verb, meaning a verb with a tense. (See **Verb tense** in the definitions below.) A clause can be *independent* (one that can stand on its own as a complete thought), or *dependent* (one that doesn't don't complete the thought). Clauses may contain phrases.

Here are some complete sentences with the dependent clause(s) in italics. The non-italicized clauses are independent ones and could stand by themselves. Some of the clauses also contain phrases. We'll discuss sentences a bit more in chapter 3.

> *If John comes home for the summer*, he will have a job building a house.

> *While he was waiting for the bus*, John saw his girlfriend with a guy dressed in a tuxedo.

> John didn't finish the job *because it was an impossible task*, and he didn't get paid for the work.

> I waited patiently *until she arrived*.

> *While she was working a fulltime job*, she attended night classes *so she could get her college degree*.

[2.2] Definitions of terms

ADJECTIVE: An adjective is a word that describes or modifies a noun (e.g., tired, angry). It can be used before the noun, *a tired cat*;

after a verb, *the cat looks tired*; with an adverb, *a very angry cat*. It can complement a noun: *Running makes the cat tired.*

ADVERB: The primary function of an adverb is to describe a verb, an adjective, or another adverb. It often answers one of several questions: *how* (carefully, quickly, horribly); *where* (there, upstairs, inside); *when* (suddenly, often, now); *how long* (continuously, briefly, forever); *how often* (frequently, rarely, ever); *to what extent* (very, too, almost, rather). (See **Conjunctive adverb**)

Many adverbs end in *ly*, but not all words ending in *ly* are adverbs. Here are some common non-adverb "ly" words.

Adjectives: lovely, timely, disorderly, friendly, unruly, heavenly, ugly, silly

Nouns: belly, bully (also a verb), family (also an adjective)

Verbs: apply, sully, bully

NOTE: A few *"ly"* words can be an adjective or adverb, depending on usage: monthly, weekly, yearly. *He pays weekly visits to his mother* (adjective). *He visits his mother weekly.* (adverb)

APPOSITIVE: An appositive is a noun or a noun phrase positioned near another noun and which renames or further defines that noun. All appositives are parentheticals (see **Parenthetical**), but the reverse isn't always true. Appositives further describe the noun, while a parenthetical may add other nondescriptive information. Appositives can fall at the beginning, middle, or end of a sentence, and they can be restrictive or nonrestrictive. (See **Nonrestrictive clause** and **Restrictive clause** for further explanations.)

The car, a Dodge Charger, sped past. (*Dodge Charger* defines the type of car.)

A former US president, Bill Clinton, is married to Hillary Clinton, first a senator from New York and later Secretary of State under Barack Obama. (*A former US president* is an appositive that precedes the noun and further defines Bill Clinton, and *first a senator... under Barack Obama* expands on Hillary Clinton.)

The speaker introduced the man next to him as Gerald Baines, a celebrated author. (*a celebrated author* adds detail about Gerald Baines.)

My younger brother, Greg, gave me a present. (*Greg* further defines *my younger brother* in a nonrestrictive way, meaning that I have only one younger brother and his name is Greg.)

My younger brother Greg gave me a present. (Here, *Greg* further defines *my younger brother* but in a restrictive way. This says that I have more than one younger brother, but Greg is the one who gave me a present.)

COMMA SPLICE: A comma splice occurs when a comma is used to separate two independent clauses without using a conjunction. This is typically considered a grammatical error, although it may be acceptable in certain situations. Here are some examples of comma splices and how to correct them. Chapter 5 will expand on this topic.

[INCORRECT]

I went to the store, I bought beer and munchies.

My brother came home from college for Christmas, he now had a beard.

Sarah admitted to having an affair with her husband's best friend, she said she would never be unfaithful again.

[CORRECT]

I went to the store. I bought beer and munchies.

My brother came home from college for Christmas. He now had a beard.

Sarah admitted to having an affair with her husband's best friend. She said she would never be unfaithful again.

COMPOUND ADJECTIVE: An adjective made up of two or more adjectives and hyphenated to make it act as one word.

blue-green car; rose-colored glasses; three-dimensional image.

Compound adjectives are different from an adjective-noun combination, which may be two words, may hyphenated by current convention, or may have merged into a single word. *Cell phone* is changing over to *cellphone*. *Website* began as *Web site* and is still used as two words in places.

COMPOUND SUBJECT: A sentence subject that has more than one noun or noun phrase to it. In the examples, the compound subject is italicized.

Jack and Jill went up the hill.

Swimming and football are my favorite sports.

Weighing myself each week and seeing how much weight I've lost encourages me to keep up my weight-loss program.

CONJUNCTION: A conjunction is a word that joins words, phrases, and clauses together. Examples: but, or, and.

CONJUNCTIVE ADVERB: Conjunctive adverbs are easier to recognize than they are to define (e.g., however, therefore, consequently, instead, likewise, meanwhile, moreover, nonetheless, otherwise). They are adverbs that provide transitions from one idea to another and often join two independent clauses. Conjunctive adverbs show cause and effect, sequence, contrast, comparison, or other relationships. The punctuation surrounding these will be discussed in chapters 6 and 9.

CONTRACTION: A contraction is a shortened form of a word or group of words. For example, *will not* becomes *won't*, *I am* becomes *I'm*, *cannot* becomes *can't*.

COORDINATING CONJUNCTION: (for, and, nor, but, or, yet, so) A coordinating conjunction joins two words, phrases, or clauses together when the items are of equal importance. The first letter of the coordinating conjunctions spells *F-A-N-B-O-Y-S*.

DANGLING MODIFIER: (See also **Misplaced modifier.**) A dangling modifier is a word, phrase, or clause whose location in a sentence leaves confusion as to what it is describing. In some cases, the object being modified is completely absent. Dangling modifiers can lead to unintended humor.

[WITH DANGLING MODIFIERS]

Hiking through the woods, the wildflowers were gorgeous. (The wildflowers were hiking? The subject being modified—the hiker—is missing.)

Running past my neighbor's house, the dog attacked me. (Who was running?)

Frustrated and tired, my bed was a welcome sight. (The bed is frustrated and tired?)

Tugging hard on the chain, it snapped. (The chain tugged on itself?)

[POSSIBLE CORRECTIONS]

Hiking through the woods, I observed the gorgeous wildflowers.

While I was running past my neighbor's house, the dog attacked me.

Because I was frustrated and tired, my bed was a welcome sight.

He tugged hard on the chain and it snapped.

DEMONSTRATIVE ADJECTIVE: (this, that, these, those) Demonstrative adjectives are used to demonstrate or point out a specific noun.

From here, that bridge appears taller than this one.

I prefer that dress.

The zoo recently acquired these llamas.

Those buildings will be demolished later this month.

DEMONSTRATIVE PRONOUN: (this, that, these, those) Like the demonstrative adjectives, demonstrative pronouns indicate a specific person, place, or thing, but instead of modifying a noun, they are used alone when the object referred to is either known or vague.

This is clearer to me now.

Who told you that?

These are beautiful paintings.

Those are more expensive cars than these.

DIALOGUE TAG: A dialogue tag is a word or words separate from the dialogue and used to denote who is speaking. Typically, the dialogue is set off from the rest of the text by quotation marks. The tag may describe how the line is spoken. We've italicized the dialogue tags in the examples below.

Sarah said, "I really don't care if he's coming or not."

"Jason refused to join us," *he said with a sigh.*

"Can't you convince him?" *Rob asked.* "I think he should be here."

"Be careful," *Jack whispered.*

GERUND: A gerund is a verb that acts like a noun. In form, a gerund is the same as the present participle of the verb (the verb + "ing" at the end). Because it is a noun, the gerund can be used as the subject or object of a verb or sentence. In the sentences below, the gerunds are shown in italics. Don't confuse a gerund phrase with a present participle phrase. A gerund phrase acts as a noun. A present participle phrase describes.

I love *swimming.*

Talking too much makes my throat dry.

Remembering the good times is usually better than *dwelling* on the mistakes of the past.

Jennifer hates *paying* the bills.

Paying the bills, Jennifer remembered this time to check her bank balance first. (Unlike in the previous example, here "paying the bills" is a participle phrase, not a gerund, because it describes Jennifer: she's paying the bills.)

INFINITIVE: An infinitive is a verb form that shows no tense or person and is commonly preceded by "to."

I like to swim. ("to swim" is the infinitive form of *swim*. See **Split infinitive**)

MISPLACED MODIFIER: Similar to a dangling modifier, a misplaced modifier is placed incorrectly in the sentence and doesn't modify or describe what it's supposed to. Unlike the dangling modifier, the subject is present either in the wrong spot, or it needs something to clarify it.

[INCORRECT]

He propped himself up in bed with a cup of coffee sitting on his chest watching the news report. (The cup of coffee is watching the news report?)

I saw the trees peeking through the window. (trees peeking?)

Freshly painted, Jim left the room to dry. (Well, it's possible that Jim had been smoking something he shouldn't have and painted himself instead of the room.)

[CORRECT]

Propped up in bed with a cup of coffee sitting on his chest, he watched the news report.

Because I have trouble sleeping, the TV helps me get through the night.

Peeking through the window, I saw the trees.

After he'd freshly painted the room, Jim left it to dry.

NONRESTRICTIVE CLAUSE: A nonrestrictive clause describes a noun or noun phrase but is not essential to the noun's description. Therefore, it is set apart by commas. (See **Appositive**.)

My cousin, who is a sophomore in college, visited me during Christmas break.

The clause *who is a sophomore in college* provides additional information about my cousin, but the clause does not define the noun. (See **Restrictive clause.**)

PARENTHETICAL: An explanatory word, phrase, or clause put in parentheses or set off with commas or dashes. (See **Appositive.**)

He was (in my opinion) unqualified for the job.

He was, in my opinion, unqualified for the job.

The sports car—a metallic blue, foreign model—caught my attention when it sped past.

Max has AB-negative blood (the rarest type).

PARTICIPLE (present, past): Participles are verb forms used as adjectives. The present participle is formed by adding "ing" to a verb (not to be confused with the gerund, which acts as a noun). The past participle is formed by adding "ed" to a verb. The English language, however, contains many irregular past participles that do not end in "ed": written, seen, gone, spoken, fallen, thought. Do not confuse the verb form with the adjective form.

She had written (verb) a letter of complaint and received a written (participle, adjective) apology from the company.

After running (gerund, noun) an exhausting (participle, adjective) marathon, Max stood under cool, running (participle, adjective) shower.

John had tripped (verb) and had fallen (verb) next to a fallen (participle, adjective) tree.

PAST TENSE: The past tense of a verb indicates action that occurred in the past of present events. (See **Verb tense.**)

He *spoke* to me yesterday.

He *ran* as fast as could to get home before it *rained*.

My dad *asked* me what I *wanted* for Christmas.

She *talked* about what she wants to do this summer.

PAST PERFECT TENSE: The past perfect tense of a verb indicates action prior to some past action.

> The rain *had stopped* (past perfect) by the time we arrived (past) home.

> Mike and I *had talked* not an hour before he disappeared.

> Greg's printer ran out of ink before he *had printed* out all of his term paper.

POSSESSIVE ADJECTIVE: (my, your, his, her, its, our, their, whose) A possessive adjective shows possession or ownership of the noun or noun phrase it refers to.

NOTE: *Whose* is both a possessive adjective and a possessive pronoun.

> Whose car is that? (possessive adjective)

> Whose is that? (possessive pronoun)

POSSESSIVE NOUN: The possessive form of a noun shows ownership of another noun. This is typically shown by adding *'s*: Jim's car. If the possessive noun already ends in "s," the current standard is to still add *'s*. (See chapter 7 on the Apostrophe.)

POSSESSIVE PRONOUN: (mine, yours, his, hers, ours, theirs, whose) A possessive pronoun is used in place of a noun to show ownership. Example: That bike is mine. *Mine* is used in place of *bike* and shows ownership.

PREFIX: A prefix is a group of letters placed at the beginning of a word to change its meaning. Example: *Unlikely* is a modified version of *likely*, with the exact opposite meaning.

PREPOSITION: A preposition is a single word that is used to link a noun, pronoun, or gerund to the rest of the sentence. In the sentence *He is going to the game*, "to the game" is a prepositional phrase clarifying where the subject is going, and "to" is the preposition.

PRONOUN: (I, you, he, she, it, we, they) A pronoun substitutes for a noun or a noun phrase in order to simplify the sentence and prevent repetition of words.

RELATIVE CLAUSE: A relative clause describes or clarifies a noun or a noun phrase. Example: The dog that bit me ran off. The clause "that bit me" clarifies which dog is being referred to.

RELATIVE PRONOUN: (who, whom, whose, which, that, whoever, whomever, whichever) Relative pronouns are used to introduce a phrase in a sentence. Example: The train that just arrived blew its horn. "That" introduces the phrase "just arrived."

RESTRICTIVE CLAUSE: A restrictive clause describes a noun or a noun phrase. It is an essential modifier because it specifies the noun and therefore is not separated by a comma. (Compare this with **Appositive**.)

My cousin who is a sophomore in college stopped by my apartment during Christmas break.

The clause specifies which cousin stopped by (the one who is a college sophomore), as opposed to some other cousin. Hence, the clause *restricts* the meaning of what it refers to. (See **Nonrestrictive clause**.)

SERIAL COMMA: This refers to the final comma (the one before *and*) in a series. In the examples below, the serial comma is shown in parentheses. (See [5.28])

Before going to work, Jim took a shower, dressed(,) and ate breakfast.

Dion, Wayne, Liam(,) and Mykel all showed up for soccer practice yesterday.

SPLIT INFINITIVE: A split infinitive refers to placing one or more words between the "to" and the verb in an infinitive (see **Infinitive**). This has been called a grammatical error, but really it is not (as explained in Chapter 1). In the following, the phrase in italics is considered a split infinitive.

Timmy likes *to happily play* with other boys his age.

to boldly go where no one has gone before (from *Star Trek*)

To properly pronounce French words requires practice.

SUBORDINATE CLAUSE: Also known as a dependent clause. (See [2.1])

SUBORDINATING CONJUNCTION: A conjunction that introduces a dependent clause is a subordinating conjunction. This clause is dependent upon the rest of the sentence for its meaning and can't stand alone as a sentence. The primary subordinating conjunctions are *although, as, because, before, even though, for, if, in order that, once, provided that, since, so that, than, that, till, unless, until, when, whenever, where, wherever, while.* (See [2.1] for examples.)

SUFFIX: A suffix is one or more letters added to the end of a word to modify its meaning. These include changing its part of speech and making a noun plural. The suffixes are italicized in the following examples: kind*ness*, careful*ly*, runn*ing*).

VERB TENSE: From the Latin for "time," the tense of a verb shows the time of its action: past, present, future (talked, was talking, talks, is talking, will talk, will be talking). These are called **finite verbs**, as opposed to nonfinite verb forms that do not show tense and do not specify time of action: infinitive, participle, gerund (to do, done, doing). (See **Past tense** and **Past perfect tense**.)

VOCATIVE: The vocative is used to denote a person, animal, or object being addressed directly. In English, set off a vocative with commas. In the examples below *James, Melissa*, and *Karl* are being addressed directly. See chapter 5 for more details on the vocative.

James, what do you think?

Come here, Melissa.

It doesn't matter, Karl, if we do it now or later.

CHAPTER THREE

PRINCIPLES OF SENTENCE STRUCTURE

Punctuation and sentence structure are tightly linked. A proper understanding of punctuation begins with understanding sentence structure.

[3.1] What is a sentence?

Depending on where you look, you will find variant definitions of a sentence. In its simplest definition, a sentence is one or more words that together form complete thought or idea and that contains a subject and a verb. The verb may show the subject acting or being acted upon. A sentence may convey a statement, question, exclamation, or command. It consists of a main clause and sometimes one or more subordinate clauses. It is the largest independent unit of grammar and begins with a capital letter and ends with a period, question mark, or exclamation point. We will discuss incomplete sentences and sentence fragments shortly.

The following are complete sentences by our definition.

Stephen cried.

Why did the car explode? (subject=car; verb=did explode)

Stop! (a command containing the implied subject *you*.)

A policeman stopped Tony for having a broken taillight. (subject is doing the acting)

Tony was stopped by a policeman for having a broken taillight. (subject is being acted upon)

[3.2] Sentence types

In school, most of us were taught three types of sentences: simple, compound, and complex. While it's nice to be able to put names to them, that doesn't really help us with learning to write.

A simple sentence has a subject (possibly a compound one), a verb (one or more) to express the subject's action, and possibly some descriptive words or phrases tossed in.

Michael listened.

John quickly told Michael the situation.

Jacob and his sister Helena drove to the store in their parents' car. (compound subject: Jacob and his sister Helena)

James drove to the store and came back home an hour later.

A compound sentence consists of two or more independent clauses joined by a coordinating conjunction.

John drove his car to the movie, and there he met two of his friends.

Mary wanted to go with John to the movie, but she was too young for its R rating.

Complex sentences include one or more dependent clauses along with an independent clause or clauses. (See [2.1] for types of clauses.)

After he finished studying, John decided to go to the movie.

"After he finished studying" is a dependent clause. The second half of the sentence is an independent clause.

John, who was nineteen, could go to an R-rated movie, but Mary, because she was only fifteen, was too young to be admitted.

This contains two independent clauses: (John could go to an R-rated movie), (Mary was too young to be admitted). They are joined by a conjunction (but). The sentence also contains two dependent clauses that don't express complete thoughts: (who was nineteen), (because she was only fifteen).

The more complex a sentence is, the more important punctuation becomes to help the reader make sense of it. Sentence structure helps govern style. Consider this sentence:

Prince Darius charged into the fight hoping to gain a victory.

An optional comma could be added after "fight" to give a slightly different emphasis. We'll discuss optional commas later in the book, but tuck the thought away for now.

Consider these variations that project different styles and moods. Note the punctuation.

Prince Darius charged into the fight, where he hoped to gain a victory.

Hoping to gain a victory, Prince Darius charged into the fight.

Into the fight charged Prince Darius, hoping to gain a victory.

Hoping to gain a victory, into the fight Prince Darius charged.

Changing sentence structure can turn a statement into a question, but changing the punctuation can do that as well.

She is going to the movie today.

Is she going to the movie today?

She is going to the movie today?

[3.3] Run-on sentences & comma splices

Whenever you join two independent thoughts (clauses), you need something to connect them. The reason run-on sentences and comma splices are said to be bad is not because someone decided they're wrong, but because such sentences do not flow properly. Run-on sentences are confusing to read because the independent clauses run together without a pause. They need to be separated.

[RUN-ON]

I have been working extra hours the last few days I fall asleep at my desk I'm so tired I miss meetings and lunch.

We stood a couple hundred yards outside the town sentries in chainmail vests patrolled the top of its walls.

[POSSIBLE FIXES]

I have been working extra hours the last few days. I fall asleep at my desk, and I'm so tired I miss meetings and lunch.

I have been working so many extra hours the last few days that I fall asleep at my desk, and I'm so tired I miss meetings and lunch.

We stood a couple hundred yards outside the town. Sentries in chainmail vests patrolled the top of its walls.

Comma splices are similar to run-on sentences. The difference is that a comma is incorrectly put where a period or conjunction should be. A pause is there, but it's the wrong kind of pause. In the examples below, we've put the splicing commas in square brackets to differentiate them from other, legitimate commas. We'll discuss commas splices further in section [5.5].

[INCORRECT]

I have been working extra hours the last few days. I fall asleep at my desk[,] I'm so tired I miss meetings and lunch.

We stood a couple hundred yards outside the town[,] sentries in chainmail vests patrolled the top of its walls.

The air was damp and thin[,] I felt myself taking deep breaths to compensate.

We don't want to dwell too much on sentence structure because this is a book on punctuation, but run-on sentences and comma splices are errors in punctuation.

Our purpose is not to teach you how to write sentences but how to punctuate them properly after they're written, and we firmly believe that once you learn proper punctuation, you'll also learn how to write better sentences that take advantage of your newfound punctuation skills.

And with that long sentence, which is neither run-on nor comma-spliced, we move on.

[3.4] Sentence fragments/incomplete sentences

We can almost hear English teachers cheering us for covering this topic, but we suspect their enthusiasm will be short-lived, and they may accuse us of grammatical anarchy. We use incomplete sentences and sentence fragments frequently in our everyday speech. A complete subject and verb aren't needed when the listener understands the context and can fill in the missing pieces. In fiction, our characters' voices must feel authentic. An uneducated street kid won't speak—or think—in complete and grammatically perfect sentences all the time. Consider this mundane, but typical conversation:

"How are you feeling today?"
"Much better."
"You going into the office?"
"Thinking about it."

All except the first line are sentence fragments. For our purposes, we'll consider sentence fragments and incomplete sentences to be the same thing since we've never found clear-cut definitions to differentiate them. Whatever you call them, they represent some part of a complete sentence.

Before you can effectively use sentence fragments, you have to know what they are and be aware that you're using them. Here are some more fragments along with an implied complete sentence.

Nice work! (That was nice work!)

Hell no. (There is no way in Hell I will do that.)

Absolutely. (I absolutely agree.)

Next right. (Take the next right turn.)

Because I felt like it. (I did it because I felt like it.)

In these examples, we knew what the speaker meant because they projected a complete thought. Although grammatically they lacked some elements of a complete sentence, and we didn't know the context, we could still fill in the blanks

Now consider some fragments that are less easily interpreted. While they make clear sense and express an idea, the unknown context makes it difficult to fill in the blanks.

That yellow Corvette racing down the street.

Annoying rat-sized dogs that nipped at my legs.

Walking into the room.

Long blonde hair framing a face with dark eyes that spoke of trouble about to happen.

Red sandstone walls with a grey slate roof and a partially covered rotted wooden conservatory that leached the heat from the building in the evenings.

Once you add a context, these fragments can work.

"When did you last see him?"
"Walking into the room."

=====

"What are you looking at?"
"That yellow Corvette racing down the street."

In our English classes, we frequently heard about sentence fragments as something we were *not* supposed to write. Ever. (Note that last fragment?)

But, guess what? In fiction we're allowed to break The Rules when it serves the story, despite what our teachers might have told us. If fiction writers always followed the formal rules of the language, we'd have a lot of stiff, dull writing in the world. (We do have that, but it's not a result of ignoring grammar.) Consider these examples:

He loved the car, and he really wanted to buy it. Except that he lacked the cash. (this works)

Dennis came home tired. Sat in front of the TV. Fell asleep there sometime after midnight. When a loud noise woke him. (The first two fragments work because they parallel the opening complete sentence. The last fragment "when a loud noise woke him" doesn't work well.)

Current convention says to capitalize fragments and end them with a period. This hasn't always been the case, and in older literature you may find exceptions.

Punctuation can turn an incomplete sentence into a complete one, can fix confusing sentences, and can change sentence meaning.

[1a] Before I did something stupid. (A sentence fragment, possibly as a reflection by the narrator on taking some preventative measure.)

[1b] Before, I did something stupid. (a statement that the narrator had already done something stupid. The comma changes the meaning, which may not be what you want.)

35

[2a] Before I had money and I lived from day to day and I was happier. (unclear meaning)

[2b] Before I had money and I lived from day to day, I was happier. (adding a comma and deleting one "and" makes it say the person was happier when poor.)

[2c] Before, I had money and I lived from day to day and I was happier. (now it says the person was happier when rich.)

Let's show two variations of [1a] in context. Note the different mood.

I figured I'd better stop before I did something stupid.

I figured I'd better stop. Before I did something stupid.

When you're in the head of a character who thinks in sentence fragments, they're acceptable. Let's look at a previous fragment example (the annoying rat-sized dogs) and make it work in context.

I put my hand on the doorknob and paused. I remembered the last time I entered this house. The pervasive mustiness. Creaky floors that sent chills up my spine. Annoying rat-sized dogs that nipped at my legs. No sooner had my hand turned the doorknob than I heard the yipping beasts.

In the following passage notice how sentence fragments create a particular mood:

I awoke—sans headache or drug hangover—to a charming déjà vu setting. To the smell of fresh air. To a night sky with two bright moons and lanterns hanging everywhere. To Jackson a few feet away. To people around me.

Angry people.

Lynch-mob people, protesting that Jackson and I were hanging in pig-roasting position, not because they thought we were being treated unfairly—gagged, naked, arms and legs aching from being cruelly lashed to our respective poles—but because the fire pits beneath us were still unlit. Jackson and I had conveniently delivered ourselves into their hands. Once again.

[3.5] Applied sentence structure

Most of us talk in simple sentences, or at most in short, complex sentences. It's natural that beginning writers will write how they

36

talk. This is exactly wrong unless you're writing dialogue. Because of this practice, writers will hear that they need to vary their sentence structure, to make some of them more complex. Unfortunately, they may interpret that to mean they should vary *all* of their sentences and make *all* of them complex. This trades one sin for another.

In the passage below, the sentence structure is varied both in style and length.

[1] Jen-Varth sat up to scan the elliptical chamber, which he judged to be one stad across and greater than that in height. The pale gray floor was smooth, stone-like but not stone. Fine dust, fresh with footprints, covered it. Ahead lay an aisle flanked by tiered rows of seats that followed the curve of the chamber. The walls glowed blue. The room reminded him of a small amphitheater. At the back, the highest tier of seats rose well above his head. He walked along the downward slope of the aisle to where it ended next to a rectangular dais. Behind it an opening led into a corridor lit with the same dim blue as the chamber walls. He followed the footprints.

Let's recast this into mostly simple and compound sentences. It's choppy, not smooth.

[2] Jen-Varth sat up to scan the elliptical chamber. He judged it to be one stad across and greater than that in height. The pale gray floor was smooth, stone-like but not stone. It was covered with fine dust. He saw fresh footprints in the dust. An aisle lay ahead. Rows of tiered seats flanked it and followed the curve of the chamber. The walls glowed blue. The room reminded him of a small amphitheater. At the back the highest tier of seats rose well above his head. He walked along the downward slope of the aisle. It ended next to a rectangular dais. Behind it an opening led into a corridor. It was lit with the same dim blue as the chamber walls. He followed the footprints.

Now let's recast most of the sentences into the same or similar structures. At first it seems fine, but when it continues paragraph after paragraph, it becomes tedious. Note the overuse of present-participle (ing) clauses. We've seen this fault in published writing.

[3] Jen-Varth sat up, scanning the elliptical chamber, judging it to be one stad across and greater than that in height. The pale gray floor was smooth, stone-like but not stone, fine dust fresh

37

with footprints covering it. Ahead lay an aisle flanked by tiered rows of seats following the curve of the chamber, the walls glowing blue. The room reminded him of a small amphitheater, the highest tier of seats at the back rising well above his head. Walking along the downward slope of the aisle and following the footprints to where they ended next to a rectangular dais, he came to an opening leading into a corridor, the same dim blue lighting the chamber walls.

The reader may not always be conscious of the reason, but closely repeated sentence structures will have a negative effect on his reading enjoyment.

[TIP] One of the best ways to avoid sentence structure problems is to read aloud what you've written. Better, have someone read it to you. Listen for repeated sentence patterns, stiff wording, places where the reader stumbles. Then revise accordingly.

With that, let's dive into the details of the various punctuation marks themselves.

CHAPTER FOUR

PERIOD, QUESTION MARK, EXCLAMATION MARK

[4.1] What is the period?

Also called a full stop, the period is the simplest and one of the oldest pieces of punctuation. It's one of the few marks that can be used together with other punctuation.

[4.1.1] Period to indicate the end of a sentence

The period is used to designate the end of a sentence, and current convention uses it to mark the end of a sentence fragment, no matter its length, as these examples show.

Someone knocked on my door. "It's open." Probably one of the two dorm stragglers coming to wish me luck with my life, although I couldn't imagine them up this early.

Off to the left, hewn rock steps carved out of the hillside led down at a hefty slope. No railing. Ahead, over a mile away, stood a hill covered with dense, green vegetation.

[4.1.2] Period in abbreviations

In abbreviations and a person's initials, a period indicates that the letter or letters represent full words (St.= Saint, Oct.= October, J. K. Rowling). Periods used to be common in most abbreviations and in some acronyms (R.S.V.P., A.W.O.L., B.C., A.D.). Many now omit the periods (AWOL, RSVP), but both forms are acceptable. B.C. and A.D. generally omit the periods.

NOTE: Unlike an abbreviation, an acronym is made up of the first letters of the words they stand for, and the result is itself a pronounceable word (e.g., NASA, NATO, AWOL, LASER—look up "laser" to see what the letters stand for). Most acronyms do not use periods today.

Many common abbreviations of all uppercase letters now omit the periods (CEO, FAA, BA, BS, PhD, US, UK, IQ, DNA, GPS, FBI, CIA), but those containing lowercase letters include the periods (a.m., p.m., Mr., Dr., e.g., i.e.).

"PhD" is an exception to be consistent with other college degree abbreviations. U.S. and U.K. still appear in some style guides, but the CMOS recommends no periods.

[4.1.3] UK variation with abbreviations

Currently in the UK it is standard practice that if the abbreviation ends with the same letter as the word it represents, no period is necessary. Thus in the UK you see *Mr*, *Mrs*, and *Dr* without periods. *Prof.* takes the period because the final "r" in *professor* is not part of the abbreviation.

[4.1.4] Punctuation & spelling in brand names

Respect the punctuation of brand names and company names. The "iPod" is spelled exactly that way. Even if it begins a sentence, do *not* capitalize the first letter, but avoid starting a sentence with it.

When using a commercial name in your writing, always verify the correct spelling and punctuation from a reliable source such the company's website. For noncommercial abbreviations, check a modern dictionary because the language changes. If the dictionaries don't list the abbreviation (check more than one dictionary), then check the CMOS or *several* online sources. Never rely on only one online source unless you know for certain that it's reliable.

[4.1.5] Period as a decimal point

When used as a decimal point, the period acts more like a spelling mark (like the apostrophe and hyphen) and does not designate a termination or pause. Many continental European countries (and not the UK), and some other countries, use a comma instead of a decimal point in numbers.

[4.1.6] Period with initials

When writing a name with initials, for the first and middle names use a period after the initial, followed by a space. When there are three or more initials (e.g., J.R.R. Tolkien), put a space only after the last initial.

[4.2] Question mark

The question mark replaces a period to indicate a direct question or an implied question, be that a sentence or a sentence fragment. Questions can be direct or indirect.

[4.2.1] Direct questions

Direct questions seek information or elaboration, ask for confirmation, or question an action or decision. Direct questions usually end with a question mark, but see [4.5] for exceptions.

How do I install that program on my computer?

Who are you?

And you are?

Did you hear what happened to Joseph yesterday?

Why should I do that?

[4.2.2] Indirect questions

An indirect question seeks information but doesn't ask for it directly. Do not use a question mark with an indirect question. When a question within a sentence is a single word (e.g., who, when, where, how, why), a question mark is not needed, and the word may be italicized for emphasis.

I wondered who she was.

Derek asked if I knew what John did to her.

He wondered what was happening.

Todd wants to know if you are going to the movie with Kristin.

The question was no longer *how* but *when*.

[4.2.3] Multiple question marks

In formal writing, you should never use more than one question mark to end a sentence. In fiction, multiple question marks signal amateurish writing. (For an exception, see [4.6.1] and see chapter 14 for better techniques than multiple question marks.)

[ILL-ADVISED USAGE]

Can we go now? Please???

What's wrong with that???

[4.3] Exclamation mark

The exclamation mark replaces a period at the end of a sentence that expresses a strong response: shouted phrases, commands, warnings, surprise, strong feelings.

As with a question mark, you should *not* use more than one to end a sentence!!! Not unless you want to look like an amateur writer. If you think of ? or ! as substituting for a period, then using more than one doesn't make sense unless you would end your sentences with multiple periods.

NOTE: The ellipsis (...) is considered a single mark, not multiple periods. (See chapter 11.)

I couldn't believe she was crying over something so stupid!

Stop!

Be careful! That metal is hot!

I told you to get back here!

[4.3.1] Historical notes on the exclamation mark

Typewriters before the 1970s did not have a separate exclamation mark above the "1" key, as do keyboards today. What was in that spot? Nothing. To type an exclamation mark, you typed an apostrophe, then backspaced and added a period below it. The exclamation mark is sometimes called a "bang." F. Scott Fitzgerald said, "An exclamation mark is like laughing at your own joke."

[4.3.2] Judicious use of the exclamation mark

Good writing practice recommends that you use the exclamation mark sparingly because its overuse can cause it to lose its effect. Although we gave examples above of possible uses of the exclamation mark, that doesn't mean you should use it everywhere it's applicable. If you find yourself relying on exclamation marks for emphasis in your writing, you're likely using it as a crutch and therefore not writing effectively.

The exclamation mark generally indicates a raised voice or shouting. If a character is shouting, that should be apparent in the writing itself. Author Tom Wolfe is famous for using it in abundance, and he has been criticized for it even though he's an established author. Such criticism would not be good for a new writer.

In dialogue, use an exclamation mark when the character is speaking in a raised voice or shouting, not when simply emphasizing a point. We will discuss various other techniques for expressing emphasis in chapter 14.

Avoid using an exclamation mark at the end of a long sentence. You don't want to make a reader wade through a long sentence before he knows it's an exclamation. If you think of exclamations as shouted words, then few people will shout a long sentence. Shaw said it best in *Punctuate It Right!*: "Most of us don't have sufficient breath to exclaim more than a few words at a time."

* * *

ADVANCED: QUESTION & EXCLAMATION MARKS

[4.4] ? and ! as substitute punctuation marks

While the question mark and the exclamation mark sometimes replace the period, they are *not* full stops by themselves. They can substitute for the period at the end of a sentence (where they do represent a full stop), but they can also replace a comma before a dialogue tag, or they can appear as extra punctuation in the middle of a sentence. (See [4.6] and chapters 12 and 15 for further explanations.)

[4.5] Nonstandard and ambiguous questions

Not all questions appear as questions with inverted word order ("she does" versus "does she") or begin with an interrogative word (e.g., what, how, why). Some sentences can be questions or statements depending on the context or the writer's or speaker's intent.

NOTE: In some of the examples below, we've put both speakers' lines in the same paragraph for convenience.

43

[4.5.1] Nonstandard question format

Sometimes a question isn't framed as a standard question.

"I played eighteen holes yesterday." "You skipped the meeting to go play golf?" (questions a decision)

"All right, get in the car." "I can go with you?" (uncertainty, asks for verification)

[4.5.2] Answering a question with a question

"Is there a chance we could meet for lunch sometime?" "How about tomorrow?" (answers the previous question by posing another question that asks for confirmation)

"You really don't want to go there?" "Why don't I?" (questions the question)

[4.5.3] Question or statement?

One way to determine the need for a question mark is whether a response is expected, although this isn't foolproof.

"I want to go skydiving on our vacation." "You're serious?" ("Are you serious?")

"I want to go skydiving on our vacation." "You're serious." (statement of surprise)

"You must be kidding. Who would blame Leo?"

"With a boss like that, who would blame Leo if he quit." (not expecting a response)

"Would you like some coffee?" "Please." (responds to the question)

"I don't care. I won't do it!" "Please?" (asks speaker to reconsider)

"How about you go on ahead and save us a spot." (a mild command)

"Why don't you start by telling me your expectations." (a mild command)

"Yesterday, Dave called his boss an idiot." "He was really stupid enough to say that?" (asks for confirmation)

"He can be so dumb at times." "Really." (agreement)

"He can be so dumb at times." "Really?" (agreement with a hint of sarcasm or perhaps saying "You're really just now noticing?)

May I take your coat and hat, sir? (asks permission)

May I take your coat and hat, sir. (offering a service)

That was satisfactory? (asking if it was)

That was satisfactory. (stating that it was)

"You don't want to go there." "I don't?"

The expression on her face when he arrived on a flying horse? Priceless! (a semi-rhetorical question)

Four variations on "why not."

"I don't think that's a good idea." "Why not?" (questions the statement)

"We should skip the meeting and go have lunch early." "Why not." (an agreement with the suggestion, no response expected)

"Do you think you'd like to work with me?" "Why not." (an affirmative response)

"Why do you want to visit Russia?" "Why not?" (questions the question)

[4.5.4] Question or exclamation?

Some questions have more the force of an exclamation. Do *not* use both a question mark and an exclamation mark. Choose the one that best expresses the line.

Do you know what Max did to her! Do you know what Max did to her?

Where do you think you're going! Where do you think you're going?

When will I ever learn!

45

What is going on here! What is going on here?

How could you. How could you? How could you!

[4.6] Exceptions to the standard usage of ? and !

Sometimes we need to step out of standard practice with these in fiction. Some of these uses are older and some are more modern.

[4.6.1] Use of multiple ? and ! marks

Although the use of multiple question marks in general makes your writing look amateurish, they can be acceptable in casual writing (e.g., personal e-mails and text messages) and it's therefore acceptable to reproduce this practice when these occur in your fiction. (See also [16.5.1])

[4.6.2] ? and ! in the middle of a sentence

In older literature, and occasionally in modern literature, the ? or ! may appear in the middle of a sentence. The first three examples below are from Mary Shelley's original *Frankenstein*. In addition to this usage of the question mark and exclamation mark, some of her punctuation (from the early 1800s) does not follow modern-day conventions. These uses show how the language changes with time and also that the "rules" are flexible.

"... and your persuasions will induce poor Elizabeth to cease her vain and tormenting self-accusations. — Poor William! he was our darling and our pride!"

"The murder discovered! Good God! how can that be? who could attempt to pursue him? It is impossible; one might as well try to overtake the winds, or confine a mountain-stream with a straw. I saw him too; he was free last night!"

"... I thought (foolish wretch!) that it might be in my power to restore happiness to these deserving people."

An energy bolt—from Aras?—flew past me, struck them, and promptly dissipated.

As he looked around the room, a woman standing by the fireplace (where did he know her from?) smiled at him.

This man—what did he say his name was? Nikolay?—exuded power.

He threw a stack of (Canadian?) bills onto the table.

Among the coins in her purse were some Mexican (?) ones.

Sometimes a writer will use a series of questions as parts of the same sentence. The first example, using lowercase for the fragments, is seen in older literature. Current convention prefers to capitalize them, but if you view the question marks as substituting for commas, the lowercase would be correct.

Allen asked, "What do you want to drink? a soft drink? coffee? beer? something stronger?"

Allen asked, "What do you want to drink? A soft drink? Coffee? Beer? Something stronger?"

[4.6.3] Question mark in parentheses (?)

A question mark in parentheses is used to indicate doubt, uncertainty, irony, or humor. We advise avoiding this technique unless no suitable alternative exists.

This technique is used in formal writing when the information (e.g., birthdates of historical figures) is uncertain, but do not use this as a substitute for looking up the information. Even in fiction, it's usually better to write the sentence differently.

William Shakespeare was born in April (?) 1564.

Joan of Arc, 1412 (?) – 1431, is considered a French heroine.

He'd heard rumors of Gerald's art collection, but a genuine (?) Picasso hanging above the fireplace stretched his credulity.

The police officer claimed he gave the suspect a mild (?) jab in stomach with his baton.

Xander Brandt claimed he was born in Germany in 1950, sixty years ago. But he didn't look a day over thirty. The only (barely legible) birth records I was able to locate showed a Xander Brandt born in 1850 (?) in Mainz, Germany.

47

Stephen told me that his uncle (Daniel Washburn?) was a fighter pilot in WWII. (The parenthetical indicates that the character is unsure of the information.)

Her (paternal?) grandfather died two years ago.

Her grandfather—paternal, I think—died two years ago. (an alternative way)

[4.6.4] Exclamation mark in parentheses (!)

As with the question mark, the exclamation mark can be used in parentheses to indicate surprise, irony, sarcasm, or humor. It may also be placed in brackets [!] instead to show irony or sarcasm. (See chapter 11 for other ways to show emphasis.)

Glenn, who weighed a hundred and fifty pounds, claimed he could eat ten (!) quarter-pound cheeseburgers and at one meal. (better to italicize "ten" and omit the !)

After Glenn told us that, Thomas said, "Really [!]"

His father, President (!) Smith, actually showed up at his college theatre production. (The exclamation expresses more surprise than italics would)

He'd heard rumors of Gerald's art collection, but a genuine (!) Picasso hanging above the fireplace? (Instead of the question mark we used in a similar example in [4.6.3], the exclamation mark shows sarcasm. Italics might be a better choice.)

[4.7] Exclamation mark overuse

Exclamation marks should be used sparingly. Some writers believe that they are the best way to show a character's excitement, but they lose their effect if overused and may be seen as a lazy way to write. Consider the passages below.

Zoe is an excitable fourteen-year-old. A few extra exclamations are acceptable.

"I'd rather we put out the usual museum pieces," Grandma told her.
"But there's a whole storeroom full of cool stuff in the east wing I'm sure no one's ever even seen!" Zoe protested.

48

"We keep them there because some of those pieces are valuable, and I don't want them damaged."

"My point exactly! People need to see them! Besides, isn't that why the cases have locks? To protect stuff?"

Drake Radley is seventeen, the only son of a wealthy businessman, and has an attitude, but the exclamation marks are used judiciously. We've used italics to stress certain words instead of putting the emphasis on the whole sentence.

"Cocktail parties *suck*!" Drake Radley flipped a finger at the full-length reflection staring back at him. He thrust his other middle up next to the first. "Times two."

He stormed out into the hall. Why didn't they make him stay in his room and study or something? Wasn't it a parental imperative to ride your kids' asses about studying? Oh no, not Ethan and Val-not-Valerie Radley. *They* had cocktail parties, and *they* expected their one and only offspring to attend them. In a *tux*!

Okay, just because it was a Saturday night, and he was a smart kid who didn't need to study much, why couldn't he just stay in his room and listen to his music? Oh, right. They'd covered that topic at dinner—

"You're part of this family, heir to the business, and you need to learn how the real world operates."

And—of course—Valerie uttered her usual line, "Your father only wants what's best for you."

"*Fine*."

[4.7] ?! and the interrobang

The combination of a question mark and exclamation mark has been used for many years by writers to indicate shocked disbelief, but this pair of marks together is also considered poor style in formal writing and is not recommended for informal or fiction writing either.

In the early 1960s, the interrobang symbol was invented as an overlay of the ? and ! marks. It gets its name from the question mark (the interrogative mark) and "bang" as an alternative name for the exclamation mark. It's a strange-looking symbol that's difficult to see in some fonts, a good reason not to use it.

The PC key code for the interrobang is ALT 8253.

It never achieved widespread acceptance and is considered a nonstandard mark. Most authorities consider it obsolete (some considered it obsolete when it was invented), but it demonstrates how the language changes to meet current needs.

SIDE NOTE: In the game of chess the combination !? denotes an interesting move, while ?! denotes a dubious move.

With regard to the use of the ?! combination, the CMOS says that if a question is really an exclamation, then use the exclamation mark. Consider the sentences below.

"You're going out with her?!" (shocked disbelief)

"You're going out with her?" (a simple question)

"You're going out with her!" (a statement)

These three sentences clearly have different meanings. How can we achieve the emphasis in the first example without using both marks?

"You're going out with *her*?"

"You're going *out* with her?"

"You're *going out* with her?

"You're really going out with her?" (mild disbelief)

"You're really going out with her." (even milder disbelief, bordering on sarcasm)

These alternatives each express different emphasis, but they are also more specific with regard to the reason for the shock or surprise, which is somewhat vague in the original.

We can use also ellipses (see chapter 11) to increase the disbelief and to shift the emphasis in a given sentence, depending on the intent.

"You're going out with... *her*?"

"You're... *going out* with her?

"You're... going *out*... with *her*?

Before you insert ?! in your writing, consider how your reader will view it and whether you might use an alternative for a stronger effect.

Here are more examples of ways to avoid the ?! marks.

"You haven't filed your taxes for the past three years?!"

"You haven't filed your taxes for the past *three* years?"

"I can't believe you haven't filed your taxes for the past *three* years!"

"The judge denied your plea for clemency?!"

"The judge *denied* your plea for clemency?"

"You did that?!"

"You did *that*?"

"You *did* that?"

"You *did* that!"

"The uncle you never knew you left you two million dollars in his will?!"

"The uncle you never knew you left you *two million* dollars in his will?"

CHAPTER FIVE

COMMA

[5.1] Purpose of the comma

The comma is the most frequently abused piece of punctuation. Using a comma instead of a period results in run-on sentences and comma splices. Failure to understand the purpose of the comma in general results in missing and misplaced commas.

If the period separates sentences, the comma separates grammatical elements within a sentence for the purpose of clarification. The most basic parts of a sentence are the subject and verb, but a sentence may also contain clauses, parenthetical elements, and appositives (defined in chapter 2). Some of these may need to be set apart. That's what a comma does.

Many pieces of punctuation have more than one use, but none is as diverse as the comma. For that reason, this is the longest chapter of our book. The comma is not that difficult to understand if you break it down into six basic uses. Learn those for now and pick up the finer points later. Using the comma properly will significantly improve your writing.

[5.2] The six basic uses of the comma

Six basic principles account for the bulk of comma usage. We will cover all of these in more detail and add others in the *Advanced* section of this chapter.

Before we begin, note that the CMOS and the AP Style Guide differ in their approach to commas. The latter prefers comma-sparse writing: only absolutely necessary commas even if the "rule" says you should put one in. While it's a good practice not to clutter your sentences with extra commas—and we'll learn when commas are optional—don't sacrifice the impact of your writing just to spare the life of a comma.

Most comma rules have exceptions, but one firm rule exists: do not place a comma between the subject and the verb in a sentence. It is grammatically incorrect to do so.

[INCORRECT]

John, ran as fast as he could to get to school before the bell rang for class. (no comma)

After sneaking out of work early to meet her boyfriend Ellen, lied to her boss the next day that she didn't feel well. (comma belongs after "boyfriend" instead of after "Ellen")

Will and Greg, hurried to get back home before their parents realized they'd gone out after dark. (no comma)

The officer found it odd that a man, stumbled into the apartment, died there, and the owner claimed not to know him. (no comma after "man")

The clouds that moments before had been white against the blue sky, unleashed a rain of black ash. (no comma, or recast the sentence: The clouds, moments before white against the blue sky, unleashed a rain of black ash.)

[5.2.1] Comma to join independent clauses

When two independent clauses are joined by a coordinating conjunction (e.g., and, but, or), use a comma *before* the conjunction. An *additional* comma may come after the conjunction in certain cases when a parenthetical follows it. (See [5.10])

[CORRECT]

John was late coming home from work. He stopped to get a burger for dinner on the way home. (two independent clauses)

John was late coming home from work, and he stopped to get a burger for dinner on the way home.

John was late coming home from work, so he stopped to get a burger for dinner on the way home.

John was late coming home from work, but he stopped to get a burger for dinner on the way home because he didn't want to eat leftovers.

John was late coming home from work. He could stop and get a burger on the way home, or he could eat at his favorite diner and enjoy the atmosphere.

[INCORRECT]

Paul hadn't touched Jeremy's things and, he hadn't called the police.

He'd tasted better wine but, it was enough to give him a light buzz and relax him.

[5.2.2] Comma after introductory elements

When a sentence begins with an introductory word (e.g., therefore, however, also), a phrase (prepositional, present participle, past participle), or a dependent clause, put a comma *after* the phrase. This includes "if-then" sentences, even if the "then" is not written. (See [5.23])

However, I don't agree with your conclusion.

Also, I suggest bringing an umbrella.

In the living room, the only light came from five candles sitting on the coffee table. (prepositional phrase)

Every time I ask her for a date, she tells me she's busy. (dependent clause)

As I scooted into the booth, I saw that Jennifer had already ordered us an appetizer.

Wherever you go from here, I'm confident that you will succeed.

If you decide to go out tonight, be sure you dress warmly. (if-then)

Arriving late at the restaurant, I looked around to see where Jennifer was seated. (present-participle phrase)

[5.2.3] Comma to separate clarifying elements

A comma separates clarifying words, descriptive phrases, incidental words, nonrestrictive clauses, appositives, and parenthetical remarks from other elements.

This is similar to [5.2.2]. The main difference is that the elements being separated occur somewhere other than at the beginning of the sentence and are not essential to the meaning of the sentence. That may sound a bit confusing, but several examples will make it clear. One way to determine whether the phrase or clause should be separated by commas is whether it can be omitted without changing the meaning of the sentence. It's not necessary to know which type of phrase it is, only that it's not an essential element of the sentence.

Let's take a simple sentence and expand it in various ways with clarifying elements in different places. In each case, the phrase or clause that is set off with commas could be deleted to leave behind a complete sentence. Because the phrases or clauses can be left out, the commas are necessary.

> Aaron and I decided to drive to the mall to check out the new clothing store.

> Aaron, my best friend, and I decided to drive to the mall to check out the new clothing store.

> Aaron and I decided to drive, instead of walk, to the mall to check out the new clothing store, even though it was only three blocks away.

> Aaron and I decided to drive to the mall, where they had some great holiday sales going on, to check out the new clothing store.

> Because I needed to update my wardrobe in order to get more dates, Aaron and I decided to drive to the mall to check out the new clothing store.

[5.2.4] Comma to separate items in a series

A comma separates items in a series.

> Vic bought bread, milk, and beer at the store.

> Blue, green, and violet are cool colors. Red, orange, and yellow are warm colors.

> Patrick spun around, drew his revolver, and aimed into the darkness behind him.

There is considerable disagreement over whether one should use the final comma (the one before "and"), which is called a *serial comma*. Much of the time it can be omitted, but sometimes it's required for clarity. The CMOS, says to insert it. Because it has been the subject of a longstanding controversy, we'll treat it at length in [5.28].

[5.2.5] Comma of direct address

A comma separates the name of a person or people being addressed directly, even if the individuals are not addressed by name. For grammar terminology aficionados, a word or phrase of direct address is termed a *vocative*. (See the definition in Chapter 2.)

Harry, will you please come into my office?

I have not decided, sir.

What's this about, Susan?

Please be seated, ladies and gentlemen, so we can begin.

I'm sorry, Miss Jackson, that we were delayed.

I'm afraid that information is confidential, Dr. Adams.

We apologize for the inconvenience, Mr. Smith, but our representative was only following our standard policy. (The comma after "Smith" doubles as the comma separating two clauses joined by "but.")

The examples below show the need for the vocative comma. Omitting it changes the meaning of the sentence from talking *to* the person to talking *about* the person.

How do you know, John? (asking John how he knows something)

How do you know John? (asking someone how he happens to know John)

I can't see, Anthony. (The speaker is blind or his line of sight is blocked.)

I can't see Anthony. (The speaker can't see where Anthony is.)

What's this about, Susan? (asks Susan what's going on)

What's this about Susan? (asks what's going on with Susan)

We can create three different meanings with comma placement.

Please stay cool guys. (unclear sentence meaning)

Please stay cool, guys. (asks the guys to stay cool)

Please, stay cool, guys. (same with different emphasis)

Please stay, cool guys. (asks the cool guys to stay)

[5.2.6] Comma with dialogue tags

A comma separates dialogue from a dialogue tag. A dialogue tag may tell *how* the words are spoken as well as who speaks them. It may include an action, but an action is not a dialogue tag.

"I really don't want to go," he said.

She said, "Will you please take off that ridiculous hat?"

"Let's sit over there, guys," Karen said and pointed at the bench.

Karen pointed at the bench. "Let's sit over there." (The first part is an action, not a dialogue tag, so use a period, not a comma, after it.)

If the dialogue is a question or an exclamation, the ? or ! replaces the comma before the tag, and the tag is *not* capitalized (unless a proper noun starts it) because the tag is part of the sentence. We discuss this in more detail in chapters 12 and 15.

"Can we eat first and get some rest first?" he asked.

"Way to go!" she cheered.

"Mrs. Radley, the gentleman from the FBI has arrived," Pete, the front desk guard, said.

***

ADVANCED: COMMA

[5.3] Restrictive & nonrestrictive clauses & phrases

[5.3.1] Clauses

Nonrestrictive means that the clause does not change or narrow the meaning of what it refers to. It's not specific and therefore it usually

57

can be omitted without significantly changing the meaning of the rest of the sentence. Set it off with commas. (See the definitions in chapter 2 for other examples.)

My car, which I drive to work when I can't ride my motorcycle, is pushing 200,000 miles. (I have a car with high mileage and a motorcycle. The "which" clause is nonrestrictive because it is incidental information.)

He visited several cities, which had been damaged by the earthquake. (The cities he visited all happened to have been damaged by the earthquake.)

Sam enjoys conversations with his friends, who believe in reincarnation. (All of Sam's friends believe in reincarnation. It's nonrestrictive because it doesn't restrict to some friends.)

He is a lawyer, who Mike dislikes. (Mike dislikes lawyers in general.)

Restrictive means the clause changes or narrows the meaning of what it refers to. It's necessary to the sentence. Do not set a restrictive clause off with commas.

The car that I drive to work is pushing 200,000 miles. (I may have more than one car, but the one I drive to work has high mileage. It restricts the meaning to a particular car.)

He visited several cities that had been damaged by the earthquake. (He specifically visited only the earthquake-damaged cities.)

Sam enjoys conversations with his friends who believe in reincarnation. (Of all Sam's friends, he specifically enjoys talking with those who believe in reincarnation.)

He is a lawyer who Mike dislikes. (Mike dislikes this lawyer, not all lawyers.)

NOTE: This last sentence is an example of letting punctuation rule sentence meaning. Follow our tip at the end of chapter 1: reword to ensure a clear meaning independent of the punctuation.

He is one lawyer that Mike particularly dislikes.

He is a lawyer, and Mike dislikes lawyers.

NOTE: In US English "which" (as a subordinating conjunction) traditionally introduces a nonrestrictive clause, while "that" introduces a restrictive one. In UK English, it is common practice to freely interchange "which" and "that." Therefore, don't rely on these words to tell you whether the clause is restrictive or nonrestrictive.

[5.3.2] Phrases

A clause contains both a subject and verb, whereas a phrase is missing one of these. As in [5.2.2], when a phrase introduces a sentence, a comma often follows it. When a present-participle or past-participle phrase occurs in the middle of the sentence, the principle of nonrestrictive/restrictive applies. If restrictive, set off with commas; if nonrestrictive, no commas.

When the participle occurs at the end of the sentence, the use of the comma depends on what the phrase modifies or whether it could be considered a parenthetical (or an afterthought). If it modifies the noun it follows, don't use a comma. If it modifies the subject of the sentence or acts as a parenthetical, use a comma.

Arriving at the airport early, Kara had time to eat before catching her plane. (intro phrase)

The person earning the highest score will win the prize. ("earning the highest score" is restrictive. Use no commas.)

Steve goes to the bar every night, drinking until it closes. (need comma because it modifies the sentence subject "Steve" not "night")

The man dancing with my wife is the groom. (restrictive)

The man in the white tuxedo, dancing with my wife, is the groom. (nonrestrictive because it doesn't specify the man. The phrase "in the white tuxedo" already did that restrictively.)

Harry watched the police arrest the man, surprised by their efficiency. (Harry is surprised)

Harry watched the police arrest the man surprised that they had caught him so quickly. (The man is surprised, restrictive)

"Hey, back off!" Jacob said, holding his hands up in front of him. (parenthetical)

59

Evan and Andrew faded into the hallway stinking of street grime and sweat. (The hallway stinks, restrictive)

Evan and Andrew faded into the hallway, stinking of street grime and sweat. (Evan and Andrew stink.)

NOTE: These last three examples also illustrate weak writing by putting participle phrases as afterthoughts at the end of sentences or after dialogue tags. Recasting such sentences, when possible, will make them stronger.

Jacob held up his hands. "Hey, back off!"

Stinking of street grime and sweat, Evan and Andrew faded into the hallway.

Evan and Andrew faded into the hallway that stank of street grime and sweat.

[5.4] Commas as pauses

A comma represents a pause, but do not insert a comma simply because you want a pause in the sentence. Make sure that the comma is permissible. Usually when you feel a pause is needed, some convention will allow you to insert a comma. Otherwise, leave it out—or find another piece of punctuation or use a sentence construction that better accomplishes your intent. Other chapters in this book will present you with those options and guidance.

Beware of using too many commas, even when they are correctly used. Comma overload can result in messy and awkward sentences. Other punctuation marks may be better options in some cases. We will show you examples as we go along.

[5.5] Comma to join two independent clauses

A comma alone should not be used to join two independent clauses. This results in a comma splice. Use a coordinating conjunction with the comma to join two independent clauses, but make sure the clauses really are independent (could stand alone as complete sentences). Just because the second clause begins with a conjunction—even if it's a long clause—does not mean it's an independent clause.

James considered buying a house instead of renting but found that the high property taxes in his area would make his monthly mortgage payment a lot more than what he could afford now.

No comma before the "but" because the clause it introduces is not independent. It's missing a subject. If you added "he" before "found" *then* you could use a comma.

[5.6] Comma to separate dependent & independent clauses

[5.6.1] Proper comma use to separate clauses

Dependent clauses are generally separated from independent ones with commas when they begin the sentence but rarely when they fall at end of the sentence. A comma may be used when the dependent clause represents a strong contrast or when emphasis is desired.

[CORRECT]

Jessica failed her exam because she didn't study for it.

Because she spent the night before at the movies and didn't study, Jessica failed her exam.

The phone rang while I was eating dinner.

The chandelier fell onto the table, while I was eating dinner. (comma used for emphasis)

Jessica failed the exam, because she chose to party the night before. (comma for emphasis)

I told him that he should leave, that it would be safer. (comma because it acts as a sort of parenthetical, and it would be awkward without the comma)

[5.6.2] Improper comma to replace a "that" or another conjunction

Do not use a comma to replace a conjunction. Sometimes in our writing we will omit "that" from the beginning of a dependent clause to make it less formal. In these examples, where "that" has been left out, do not put a comma in its place because then we've created a comma splice.

[INCORRECT]

The air was so thin, he could hardly breathe.

She was so relieved that his idea worked, she wanted to kiss him.

[CORRECT]

The air was so thin that he could hardly breathe.

She was so relieved that his idea worked that she wanted to kiss him.

She was so relieved that his idea worked. She wanted to kiss him.

[INCORRECT]

Dad even bought the tickets for me, he was so glad his son was finally going on a date.

[CORRECTED]

Dad even bought the tickets for me. He was so glad his son was finally going on a date.

Dad even bought the tickets for me because he was so glad his son was finally going on a date.

Dad was so glad his son was finally going on a date that he even bought the tickets for me.

NOTE: A semicolon would not be appropriate here because the clauses are not sufficiently connected or parallel. (See [6.2])

[5.7] Comma to separate a series of adjectives

When two or more adjectives equally describe the same noun, they are called coordinate adjectives) and they are separated by commas. This use is trickier than in a simple series. The hard part is defining what "equally describe" and "coordinate" mean.

[5.7.1] Coordinate sentence elements

Sentence elements are coordinate if they are equal in function in every way and their order doesn't matter. This is where the term *coordinating conjunction* (e.g., and, but, or) comes from. It coordinates—joins—two equal items. In these examples, note how we can flip the clauses and the meaning doesn't change.

He watered the lawn, and he washed his car.

He washed his car, and he watered the lawn.

He wanted to water the lawn as well, but he had to wash his car first.

He had to wash his car first, but he wanted to water the lawn as well.

[5.7.2] Tests for coordinate adjectives

To demonstrate, consider "a man's left hand that's wrinkled." The adjectives (wrinkled, left, man's) are coordinate because we can place them in any order and still have them make sense, even if some sequences seem better than others.

a man's, wrinkled, left hand
a left, man's, wrinkled hand
a wrinkled, man's, left hand

Another test of coordination is whether we can put "and" between the adjectives and have them still make sense: wrinkled and a man's and left. If "and" makes sense, the comma is correct.

But if we omit one comma and write "a left, wrinkled man's hand" we've removed the coordination between "wrinkled" and "man's." Now we're saying that the hand belongs to a wrinkled man.

If we write "a wrinkled, man's left hand," then we don't need the comma after "man's." Is there a difference in meaning between "man's, left hand" and "man's left hand"? No. Therefore, the comma is not necessary. Even though the "rule" says to use commas between all of the adjectives, as long as the sentence is perfectly clear, we can omit unnecessary commas to avoid comma clutter.

Look at this pair, both correct but with different meanings.

He wore a light, blue, dress shirt.

He wore a light blue, dress shirt.

In the first case (coordinate adjectives), the shirt is blue and light (lightweight). In the second (noncoordinate adjectives), the shirt is light blue in color.

Short, kinky, black hair came to a point on his forehead.

Short, kinky black hair came to a point on his forehead.

The adjectives (short, kinky, black) are all coordinate, but there's no chance of misunderstanding the meaning. We can leave out the comma after "kinky." Unlike the blue shirt example where "light, blue" and "light blue" are different descriptions, "kinky black" and "kinky, black" are not.

A large brown spider crawled over the orange autumn leaf.

We have two sets of adjectives here ("large" and "brown"; "orange" and "autumn"), but they are not coordinate. While we can put "and" between them (one test of coordination), when we flip them, they don't feel natural. "Large" modifies "brown spider" more than it modifies "spider," and "orange" ties more closely to "autumn leaf" than to just the leaf. Switching the adjectives—or putting "and" between them—creates awkward sentences. No commas are needed in the original.

[AWKWARD] A brown large spider crawled over the autumn orange leaf.

[AWKWARD] A large and brown spider crawled over the orange and autumn leaf.

An example with three adjectives will reinforce this.

a cold sterile marble hallway (Where do we insert commas?)

[AWKWARD] a marble cold sterile hallway

[CORRECT] a cold, sterile marble hallway

[CORRECT] a sterile, cold marble hallway

Here are more examples of where commas are not required.

the big bad wolf
a shiny new car
a bright full moon
a purebred Siberian Husky

64

[5.8] Commas in pairs

Commas often occur in pairs to set off a phrase or clause, but sometimes one of the pair will invisible for one of two reasons:

(1) It would fall at the start of a sentence.

(2) It's replaced by, or absorbed by, another piece of punctuation (e.g., period, dash—see chapter 10 for dashes).

> David, because he studied hard, pulled A's and B's in all his courses.

> Because he studied hard, David pulled A's and B's in all his courses. (first comma falls at start)

> Despite the best intentions, no man or woman—not even the most disciplined, not in the course of a few weeks or months—is going to change a deeply ingrained habit. (an expected comma after "months" is absorbed by the dash)

> Cyrus was forty years old, only twenty years a vampire, and already he showed a level of intelligence that made anything possible for him. (normal parenthetical set off with commas)

> Cyrus was forty years old, only twenty years a vampire—and already he showed a level of intelligence that would make anything possible for him. (comma absorbed by a dash)

Commas of direct address display the same pair behavior.

> Please, Michael, join us for dinner.

> Michael, please join us for dinner. (comma falls at start)

> Please join us for dinner, Michael. (comma absorbed by period)

The exception to comma pairs is with a series, where the commas are individual and used as needed.

[5.9] Comma before "as" clauses

We see writers sometimes inserting incorrect commas before "as" clauses in sentences.

"As" can have two different meanings. One uses the comma; the other does not. When "as" means "while" or "during" (in the sense of "in the same way or at the same time"), don't use a comma. When it means "because" or "just like." it's treated like a parenthetical remark.

If the "as" clause begins the sentence, treat it like any introductory phrase and use a comma, regardless of the meaning of "as."

[INCORRECT]

Evan slid the key into the lock, as he looked around to see if anyone was watching.

Angela listened to the radio, as she cooked breakfast as she always did every Saturday morning.

[CORRECT]

Evan slid the key into the lock as he looked around to see if anyone was watching. (=while)

Angela listened to the radio as she cooked breakfast, as she always did every Saturday morning. (1st=while; 2nd=just like)

As he looked around to see if anyone was watching, Evan slid the key into the lock. (introductory clause)

John couldn't drive his car, as he had it in the shop for repairs. (=because)

It seemed to be a foregone conclusion that they would hook up, as they had already both declared their mutual attraction. (=because)

Ted's father, a career-Army man, expected his son to join the Army, as his brother Simon had done. (=just like)

"As" clauses often result in weaker sentences (and many writers overuse them). Avoid ones that mean "at the same time" unless the actions are simultaneous. Consider these alternatives.

Before Evan slid the key into the lock, he looked around to see if anyone was watching.

Because John had his car in the shop for repairs, he couldn't drive it this week.

[5.10] Comma after conjunctions for parentheticals

We told you earlier in this chapter that you shouldn't put a comma directly *after* a coordinating conjunction.

Most of the time that's a good practice, but, as we'll see, there are exceptions.

"As we'll see" in this example is a parenthetical comment that would normally be separated by a pair of commas. Some authorities say to omit the comma after the conjunction because it's unnecessary. It also overstuffs the sentence with commas, and visually it can be confusing. It's acceptable either way. When the parenthetical is long, the extra comma may make the sentence clearer.

I never see Edward studying because he claims he has a photographic memory, but, and here's the thing that really puzzles me, he forgets easy things like birthdays.

Sometimes the extra comma creates a different mood that may be desirable.

TIP: To emphasize a parenthetical or to set it off more, use dashes instead of commas. (See [10.6.2])

I never see Edward studying because he claims he has a photographic memory, but—and here's the thing that really annoys me about him—he forgets easy things like birthdays.

Normally, don't put a comma after a conjunction unless a parenthetical follows and you want to emphasize it, but be alert for comma clutter. (See also [5.29] on optional commas.)

[INCORRECT] (put the comma *before* the conjunction)

He went to the store for a six-pack of Coke and, he bought two cases of Pepsi instead.

He went to the store for a six-pack of Coke but, he bought a six-pack of beer instead.

[ACCEPTABLE] (but use sparingly)

Kevin makes more money than I do and doesn't have a family to support. But, he's always asking me to pay for lunch whenever we go out.

67

When Ted drove him to the store to buy beer, Jeff realized he'd left his wallet and driver's license at home. And, Ted was underage.

However, some conjunctions (e.g., or, so, yet) almost invite commas after them because a pause feels natural, particularly in dialogue.

[ACCEPTABLE]

You can have both suits for $200. Or, you can buy just one for $150.

So, are we doing this or not?

Al's car is only six months old. Yet, he's always taking it into the shop for something.

[5.11] Comma to join independent clause & fragment

The rules say not to join an independent clause and a fragment with a comma, but sometimes we may add one to emphasize the second clause. When the sentence is long and the second clause or fragment is incomplete, but long, we may add a comma to make it easier to read. Do not confuse this usage with a comma splice, which joins complete sentences with a comma.

She entered the room and stopped. (normal sentence)

She entered the room, and stopped. (added for emphasis)

Kyle left the house, and he returned forty minutes later with his girlfriend. (normal sentence, two independent clauses joined with a conjunction and comma)

Kyle left the house and he returned forty minutes later. (same as above, comma omitted so the two events flow together)

Kyle left the house and returned forty minutes later with his girlfriend. (independent clause and a fragment, no comma)

Kyle ran out of the house, and returned out of breath a minute later. (comma added to emphasize the second event)

The fantastic New Year's Eve buffet at Gino's restaurant always delighted its loyal patrons, and taxed their agility to navigate a course around the tables to the serving stations. (comma not required but used to break up the sentence and to emphasize the second half. We could make it into two independent clauses by adding "it" before "taxed.")

[5.12] Comma to show contrast

When a phrase beginning with a conjunction (e.g., but, not, yet) shows a contrast, set the phrase off with commas.

Eric told him that I would help him move, not do it all for him.

I expected that I would meet my new boss, not his assistant, my first day on the job.

At the audition I was nervous, but hopeful, that I'd get the part.

The work was difficult, yet rewarding.

Compare those with the following example where there's no contrast with "but not all of it." One could still use a comma for emphasis.

After the air conditioner broke on that sweltering day, opening the windows alleviated some of the discomfort but not all of it.

[5.13] Comma after introductory elements

We briefly discussed the use of commas with introductory words, phrases, and clauses in [5.2.2] under the six basic uses of the comma, but let's expand on that.

[5.13.1] Exclamatory and introductory words

A comma usually follows exclamatory and introductory words (e.g., oh, ah, yes, no, well) unless the word is part of a phrase or paired with another similar word, or we want the extra pause.

If the introductory word is an integral part of the sentence, instead of being a separate response, you may omit the comma, as in the examples marked ** below).

When the "Oh" of direct address (the "vocative Oh") is used, do not put a comma after it. (See [5.14] below.) The single vocative "O" is considered more poetic, but obsolete. If used, capitalize the "O" even in the middle of a sentence. (See [5.27])

Oh, you're absolutely correct.

Oh mighty one! (vocative Oh—no comma)

Bless me, O Great Spirit!

Ah, here we are.

Yes, that's correct.

** Yes that's correct.

Ah yes, that's the case.

Ah, yes, that's the case. (different emphasis)

Well, I should have expected that.

** Well I should have expected that.

** No you can't go!

Well, then maybe we should reconsider the previous plan.

When the introductory word is an adjective, use a comma to avoid an awkward sentence.

Humiliated, he left the meeting.

Excited, she wasted no time in accepting his marriage proposal.

Nervous, Dave forgot several of lines the first night of the play. (without the comma it nicknames him "Nervous Dave.")

[5.13.2] Comma with various introductory phrases

Introductory infinitive phrases, participle phrases, gerund phrases, prepositional-gerund phrases, and adjective phrases all generally take a comma after them.

To succeed in life, you need a good education. (infinitive)

Stumbling through the woods, he finally found the main road. (gerund)

On hearing of his brother's death in combat, he immediately called his parents. (prepositional-gerund)

Old and rusty, Peter's car still gets him where he needs to go. (adjective)

Exhausted from trekking through snow, Greg returned home without having shot a single buck. (participle)

Don't confuse introductory phrases with the subject of the sentence, and don't separate a subject phrase from the verb with a comma.

[CORRECT]

Tapping my fingers on the table annoyed my sister to no end.

To win the Nobel Prize had been his goal for many years.

[INCORRECT]

Tapping my fingers on the table, annoyed my sister to no end.

To win the Nobel Prize, had been his goal for many years.

[5.13.3] Optional comma after introductory elements

Sometimes the comma after an introductory element is optional, especially with short prepositional phrases or with phrases that are displaced in the sentence from their normal position. This optional comma may still be inserted to alter the emphasis or when needed for clarity. Optional commas are indicated (,).

Into the woods he went.

From here(,) where do we go?

Without your help(,) I don't know if I can do this.

In turn(,) they were asked which team they wanted to be on.

An hour later(,) Pete returned.

In keeping with our stated goals(,) we all agreed to continue.

Unlike you(,) I don't lose my temper over insignificant things.

I don't lose my temper, unlike you, over insignificant things.

To be or not to be, that is the question.

With me on your side(,) you might get through this.

You might get through this with me on your side.

With me(,) you have a chance. With him(,) you'll fail.

Unfortunately(,) he acted on advice that turned out to be bad.

Then what's it matter when we leave?

Then(,) it began to rain harder.

With your permission(,) I will leave now.

In the fall(,) we're planning a trip to Europe.

On my way out of the kitchen(,) I grabbed a donut.

After eating, my brother went to Kevin's house. (needs the comma to avoid being misread)

The day after, my sister showed up wanting to borrow money. (Without the comma, it's a sentence fragment and has a different meaning.)

When a series of prepositional phrases comes at the beginning, do not separate them individually unless they form a distinct series.

Under some old shirts at the bottom of the drawer(,) he found his passport. (one set of prepositional phrases that forms a unit, so only one comma, and that one is optional)

At the bottom of one drawer, under some old shirts, he found his passport. (The comma after "drawer" avoids an awkward sentence. "Under some old shirts" can also be viewed as a parenthetical phrase requiring commas to separate it.)

Over the river, into the woods, to Grandma's house they went. (a series)

[5.14] Comma with conjunctive adverbs

We can't give you a hard rule on this one because conjunctive adverbs sometimes act as simple adverbs instead of conjunctions, and the punctuation changes depending on which role they play. Conjunctive adverbs can be a single word or an adverbial phrase. (See also chapter 6.)

accordingly, also, anyhow, anyway, besides, certainly, consequently, conversely, eventually, finally, furthermore, hence, however, incidentally, indeed, instead, ironically, likewise, meanwhile, moreover, namely, nevertheless, next, nonetheless, now, otherwise, perhaps, rather, similarly, still, subsequently, then, thereby, therefore, thus, unfortunately, yet

as a result, as a consequence, at last, at the same time, for example, for instance, in addition, in any case, in fact, on the contrary, on the other hand, that is

A conjunctive adverb represents a transition or link between thoughts. As such, it's also an interruption and is therefore separated from the rest of the sentence with commas. However, when the interruption is weak, do not use a comma to separate it.

NOTE: The previous paragraph contains three conjunctive adverbs: *as such, therefore, however.* Pay attention to the punctuation around them.

In the following examples, we've noted the word's role (conjunctive or simple adverb) and whether it creates a weak break.

However, I still disagree with you. (conjunctive)

I still, however, disagree with you. (conjunctive)

However you do it, don't tell anyone. (simple)

Nevertheless, I reserve the right to change my mind. (conjunctive)

I nevertheless reserve the right to change my mind. (conjunctive, weak)

You therefore require a good set of tools to get the job done. (conjunctive, weak)

Therefore, you require a good set of tools to get the job done. (conjunctive)

Don't tell John, however you decide to do it. (simple adverb, but comma needed because it's a parenthetical)

I had planned on going home. Instead, I went to the bar. (conjunctive)

I went to the bar instead. (conjunction, weak)

The contract was not in Sam's best interest. He chose, therefore, not to accept the offer. (Commas are optional depending on the desired emphasis.)

[5.15] Comma before terminal adverbs

Normally we separate adverbs (e.g., too) and adverbial phrases *only* when they come at the beginning of a sentence, not when they occur at the end of it. There's a longstanding convention that a comma should precede "too" at the end of a sentence, but this comma is unnecessary. Many editors will add the comma, while others will take it out. The trend is moving toward leaving it out.

I want to go(,) too.

That was my thought(,) as well.

John felt that she should still go to the dance with him(,) though.

[5.16] Commas in dates

When a date has two or more parts, use a comma to separate the parts when the parts both are words or both are numbers. If a full date does not end the sentence, follow the year with a comma. Use no comma between the month and day and no comma if a preposition connects parts of the date. When a date is inverted as day, month, year, do not use commas to separate the elements.

She was born July 29, 1953.

He died on July 4, 1976, in New York City.

The meeting will take place on Thursday, August 6.

Barry graduated from Yale University in May 1977.

On a Wednesday in October 1946, he came into the world. (no comma after "Wednesday" because of the preposition, but need one after 1946 because it's part of an introductory clause.)

The last time we visited his parents was August 1998 for their thirtieth wedding anniversary. (no commas here)

Our recent mayor was elected on 4 November 2012 in a landslide victory.

When a full date used as an adjective, authorities disagree on whether to put a comma after it. To avoid the problem, recast the sentence, as in the second example.

The January 24, 2014(,) meeting was cancelled due to predicted snowstorm.

The meeting scheduled for January 24, 2014, was cancelled due to a predicted snowstorm.

If you wonder why a comma should follow a full date, think of the year as an appositive that clarifies which month and day in the year. Do not confuse this with a comma incorrectly separating a subject and verb. Thus, if you delete the year, remove the comma after the 24.

The meeting scheduled for January 24 was cancelled due to a predicted snowstorm.

[5.17] Commas in geographic references

Use commas to separate the elements in a geographic reference. When the final element appears in the middle of a sentence, follow it with a comma. A geographic element is defined as the name of the individual city, town, county, state, country, etc., even if the name consists of more than one word. As with dates, the elements in geographic references are all appositives and are therefore surrounded by commas.

Do not put commas after street numbers or between the state and postal code. A comma will follow the postal code only if it occurs in the middle of a sentence.

Jeff's family moved from London, England, to San Diego, California, last year.

Brian currently lives in Atlanta, Georgia, USA, but he was born in Sydney, New South Wales, Australia, and lived there until he was twelve.

I live at 333 Magnolia Street, Canton, Ohio 44444, in a blue house.

[5.18] Commas in names of people & businesses

Do not use commas before Jr., Sr., II, III, etc., in a person's name unless the name is inverted.

Do not use commas before business name designations (e.g., Inc. and Ltd.).

> I met John Smith Jr. in college before he took over Acme Stone and Gravel Inc. from his father, John Smith Sr. Naturally, he named his son John Smith III.

> I wrote my name on the form as they asked: Doe, John, Jr.

[5.19] Comma with "not only...but also" clauses

Commas are usually not necessary with such expressions unless special emphasis is required. Note that this refers to dependent clauses and phrases. Use a comma with independent clauses.

> We brought not only beer, wine, and munchies to the party but also soft drinks for the designated drivers.

> He carried so many credit cards around that he needed not one but two wallets to hold them.

> She always made reservations months in advance of when most people did—not only to be sure of the reservation, but also to be sure she got the best seats. (comma for emphasis)

> For our trip to New Mexico, Brody not only packed lightweight clothing, but he also packed heavier things because he heard it got cold at night there sometimes. (independent clauses)

[5.20] Comma with "the more...the less" expressions

Separate the clauses with a comma unless they're short.

> The more I'm forced to work extra hours, the less I enjoy it.

> The more the merrier.

> The less you worry the better.

> The less you care about what others think of you, the better off you are.

76

[5.21] Comma between repeated words

Use commas between repeated words only when clarification seems necessary or you wish to add a pause for emphasis. It's usually wise to reword to avoid such pairings.

The wedding party members lined up and walked in, in pairs.

Whatever is, is good.

The problem with wine is, is if I had had less of it, it wouldn't have made me sick. (The "had had" is all one verb, so no comma there.)

[BETTER] The problem with wine is that if I had had less of it, then it wouldn't have made me sick.

[5.22] Comma with appositives & parentheticals

[5.22.1] Appositive and parenthetical similarities

We talked about appositives previously and treated them similar to clauses in terms of being restrictive or nonrestrictive. Often the appositive adds parenthetical or nondefining information. In these cases, set it off with commas as if it were nonrestrictive.

Dr. Jacobs, a respected surgeon, is joining the staff at St. Mary's hospital.

Derek Harrison, an expert in Ancient Near Eastern archaeology, has written several award-winning novels set in Ancient Egypt.

Her brother Craig is a vegetarian. Her other brother, Nate, is a devout meat-a-tarian. ("Craig" is a restrictive appositive because it specifies which brother. "Other brother" says that she only has two brothers, so the second appositive "Nate" is nonrestrictive. Without the commas around "Nate" it says she has two brothers named Nate.)

My brother, Jason, is the smart one in the family. (one brother)

My brother Jason is the smart one, my brother Michael not so much. (more than one brother, so these names are restrictive— no commas)

[5.22.2] Appositive and parenthetical differences

Often, appositives and parentheticals are treated the same way. Both can add information. The difference is that an appositive further describes the noun, but a parenthetical is less limited.

> I recently read Shakespeare's tragedy *Macbeth*.

No comma is used after "tragedy" because it's restrictive. With a comma, it would say that Shakespeare wrote only one tragedy, and it was *Macbeth*.

[5.22.3] Appositive as part of a proper name

If the appositive is part of a proper name, do not set it off with commas.

> Richard the Lion-hearted
> John the Baptist

[5.22.4] Appositives set off with dashes

Appositives can be set off with dashes instead of commas for emphasis. Refer to chapter 10 for information on the em-dash.

> As of January 2014, four of the past five US presidents—Jimmy Carter, George H. W. Bush, Bill Clinton, and George W. Bush—were still alive.

> On the top shelf, just above his head, stood ten narrow volumes—journals—one for each of the past ten years.

> The name of Karaydeon—a name at the edge of legend—was inscribed above the portal.

[5.22.5] "Such as" with appositives

When "such as" introduces an appositive, it is *never* followed with a comma or a colon.

> [CORRECT] Classic vampires have certain weaknesses, such as repelled by garlic, fear of crosses, burn up in sunlight.

> [INCORRECT] Classic vampires have certain weaknesses, such as, repelled by garlic, fear of crosses, burn up in sunlight.

[INCORRECT] Classic vampires have certain weaknesses, such as: repelled by garlic, fear of crosses, burn up in sunlight.

[5.22.6] An appositive cannot be a sentence

[CORRECT] I owe my life to one special person, my brother.

[CORRECT] I owe my life to one special person: my brother.

[INCORRECT] I owe my life to one special person. My brother. (an awkward sentence fragment)

[5.23] Commas in if-then sentences

If-then sentences should always insert the comma after the *if* clause. These sentences begin with a subordinate clause, so the comma is required, even if "then" is missing. Some may consider this comma optional, but it really should be inserted.

[CORRECT]

If we go to the movie tonight, then Alan won't be able to come.

If we go to the movie tomorrow, Jane won't be available.

[INCORRECT] If you go to the movie Sunday I can't make it.

[5.24] Comma after parentheses

If a comma would normally be used in a sentence in the absence of parenthetical material, a comma follows the text in parentheses. Test this by deleting the parenthetical material. If a comma would be needed for other reasons, insert it.

[CORRECT]

Ted showed up at the party with my old girlfriend, much to my surprise, and introduced her as his fiancée.

Ted showed up at the party with my old girlfriend (much to my surprise) and introduced her as his fiancée. ("much to my surprise" is already parenthetical, so no extra commas)

Ted showed up at the party with my old girlfriend (much to my surprise), who didn't look happy about it.

Ted showed up at the party with my old girlfriend (much to my surprise), but she didn't look happy to be there.

With my old girlfriend in tow (much to my surprise), Ted showed up at the party.

[5.25] Comma with "that is" & "namely" expressions

When certain words or phrases of the "that is" type precede a list of appositives (e.g., that is, namely, for example), a comma typically follows the word or phrase. Use dashes or parentheses to create a more readable sentence.

At the university I attended as an undergraduate, several of the courses for freshman engineering students, namely, Elementary Functions, Calculus I, and Freshman Chemistry caused many of those students to switch to a business major.

At the university I attended as an undergraduate, several of the courses for freshman engineering students—namely, Elementary Functions, Calculus I, and Freshman Chemistry—caused many of those students to switch to a business major.

In addition to his wife's diamond jewelry, his safe contained uncut diamonds, three passports with his picture (that is, in three different names), a German Luger, and stacks of foreign currency—specifically, Russian, German, Finnish.

When "or" in the sense of "that is" (to mean "in other words") introduces a phrase, set that phrase off with commas.

During our walk in the woods, Riley pointed to a plant growing around the trees. "*Toxicodendron radicans*, or poison ivy, is the bane of many hikers."

NOTE: When the Latin abbreviations for "for example" (e.g.) and "that is" (i.e.) are used in formal writing, they should be confined to parentheses and followed by a comma, as we have done throughout this book.

She loves decadent desserts (i.e., anything containing excessive sugar, butter, and chocolate).

For crunchy snacks, Craig prefers vegetables (e.g., celery, carrots, radishes) over chips and crackers.

[5.26] Comma with "such as" and "including"

Phrases introduced by these are set off with a comma when nonrestrictive, but with no comma when restrictive.

[CORRECT]

He loves movies such as *Star Wars*. (restrictive because he does not love all movies, just those like *Star Wars*)

He loves sci-fi adventure movies, such as *Star Wars* and *Transformers*. (nonrestrictive because he loves all movies of that type, and these are merely two examples).

Examples such as this are exceptions to the rule. (restrictive, refers to only certain examples)

She likes to cook with aromatic spices, including oregano and cumin. (nonrestrictive)

[5.27] Notes on the vocative

Some languages use a special form of the noun for the vocative case. A familiar example is the line "Et tu, Brute?" in Shakespeare's *Julius Caesar* where *Brute* is the vocative form of *Brutus* and shows Brutus as the one being addressed. The comma after *tu* is modern. The Latin of the day did not use commas or periods, and the vocative precludes the need for a comma anyway.

The only surviving forms of the vocative in modern English occur in Biblical and poetic expressions where the "O" is written as a single letter to distinguish it from "Oh!" as an exclamation. Modern usage usually substitutes "Oh" for the vocative "O."

O ye of little faith (the Bible, Matthew 8:26)

O death, where is thy sting? (the Bible, 1 Corinthians 15:55)

To what green altar, O mysterious priest (John Keats, "Ode to a Grecian Urn")

[5.28] The serial comma controversy

The serial comma (the comma before "and" after the last item in a series) is also known as the Oxford or Harvard comma (from different sides of the Atlantic Ocean). The controversy over its use has been going on for decades. Most of the time this comma is not necessary, and even the style guides do not agree on its use. The AP Style Guide says no; the 16th edition of the CMOS recommends it, a change from previous editions. Many editors leave it out except when required for clarity. We prefer to insert it because most of the time it makes the sentence cleaner to read.

> Ryan walked into the room and saw a dead body on the floor, the medical examiner photographing the body, and two policemen standing nearby.

What did Ryan see? He saw the dead body, but if you leave out the comma after "body," it says that he saw the medical examiner photographing the body and the two policemen. Omitting the comma in this case leaves the sentence open to misinterpretation or unintended humor.

Here is a famous example to support the serial comma. What if a student gave this dedication?

> I'd like to thank my parents, the Pope and the Virgin Mary.

With the serial comma missing, what follows the comma could be seen as an appositive to "parents." Critics of the serial comma claim that such examples are exceptions and that no reasonable person would misinterpret them.

> My duties include answering phone calls, responding to e-mails, filing and supervising employees. (He supervises and files employees?)

> Among those interviewed were his two ex-wives, Kris Kristofferson and Robert Duvall. (taken from a newspaper article about Merle Haggard)

In this day and age when gay marriages are permitted, you probably don't want to risk the misinterpretation in that last example. A simple serial comma avoids these potential problems.

Proponents say to use the serial comma because it avoids ambiguity and matches spoken cadence (we naturally pause after each element in a series). Opponents claim it's redundant. Whichever approach you choose, always make sure your sentences are clear and not open to grammatical interpretation. The careful writer must remain alert at all times.

Some sentences are still ambiguous even with the serial comma.

They went to Oregon with Betty, a maid, and a cook.

Is "a maid" an appositive describing Betty, or the second in a list of three people. Removing the serial comma doesn't help because it leaves the possibility that Betty is both a maid and a cook.

They went to Oregon with Betty, a maid and a cook.

In this case, reword the sentence to ensure the intended meaning.

[1 person]

They went to Oregon with Betty, who was a maid and a cook.

They went to Oregon with Betty, their maid and cook.

[2 persons]

They went to Oregon with Betty—a maid—and a cook.

They went to Oregon with a cook and Betty, a maid.

[3 persons]

They went to Oregon with Betty, as well as a maid and a cook.

They went to Oregon with Betty, one maid, and a cook.

[5.29] When are commas optional?

We've already discussed optional commas in several places, but let's summarize. First, let's look at where commas are absolutely required: direct address, certain date formats, to separate items in a series (except the last item), with nonrestrictive clauses (to avoid misreading), and to separate dialogue from dialogue tags (unless you're using a nonstandard method of dialogue).

Everywhere else, they are *potentially* optional. So, are those six basic comma rules we gave at the start of this chapter meaningless? Absolutely not. While commas are correct in all of those cases, they're not always necessary.

We wish to emphasize that "potentially optional" does not mean you can ignore those commas. It's fine to adopt a comma-sparse style of writing, but don't compromise the clarity of your writing. Taking a "let's be environmentally responsible and conserve punctuation" approach can alienate your readers just as much as being a punctuation litterbug will.

In the following examples, the commas in parentheses are not needed even though the rules say to use them. Adding these commas may alter the feeling of the sentence, and that change may not be in line with the writer's intent. These example sentences are completely clear without the commas and the reader is not likely to stumble.

In my opinion(,) it doesn't matter.

When George got to the theatre(,) Pam was already there.

On Saturday(,) he went to the car dealer(,) and he bought a new car.

Public baths(,) like the ones on the hills of Rome(,) were common in all Roman cities and conquered lands.

Officially(,) I work for the government.

He needs immediate medical help(,) or he'll die.

In June(,) I will look for a new job.

No matter how often you tell me(,) or how many presents you give me, I always know you love me.

Brian knelt on the pavement(,) next to the railing and bars that separated him from the water(,) and watched the boat leaving without him.

I am aware of the money that has come into your possession(,) and I am proposing a partnership that will increase your wealth and protect you and your interests as well as mine.

He noted that the young man spent serious time at the gym(,) and that might provide an opportunity for casual conversation where he might gain additional information.

Sometimes the reverse is true. A comma may not be called for by the rules, but its addition adds a different flavor or is needed to avoid confusion. In these examples, the indicated comma (,) normally would not be necessary, but using it gives a possibly desirable pause.

She's very shy(,) but very nice.

I finished grad school at twenty-five, met your Dad after you started college, and(,) four years later, here I am dragging his son into the depths of my depravity.

Exhausted by his efforts, he slid down the wall(,) and passed out.

He pulled out the arrow and he let the blood flow freely(,) to cleanse the wound.

[5.30] Acceptable comma splices

In chapter 2 we defined the comma splice, and we discussed it chapter 3. Every English teacher and grammar guru on the planet will tell you that a comma splice is a mortal sin. High school and college English courses drill that into us.

Why are comma splices considered wrong? For one, they may indicate the writer's inability to understand what a sentence is. For another, they can cause a sentence to be misread.

Several of his friends and he went to the movie matinee, since he hadn't eaten lunch, he bought a hot dog at the theatre.

This could be misread initially that he went to the movie because he hadn't eaten lunch and might cause a reader to go back over it to understand the meaning. It's generally bad when readers have to re-read a sentence. Here, the first comma should be a period.

Commas splices can sometimes yield a more effective sentence, but you should be aware that using them is risky because it may cast your writing in a bad light to some readers.

Here are some famous, and often cited, comma-spliced sentences.

I came, I saw, I conquered.

Man proposes, God disposes. (from Strunk and White's, *Elements of Style*)

Think like a man of action, act like a man of thought. (Henri Bergson)

The pleasures of the intellect are permanent, the pleasures of the heart transitory. (Henry David Thoreau)

This was not only his first concerto, it was his best. (Wilson Follett, author of *Modern American Usage*)

Follett suggests that comma splices may be used in "not only...but also" constructions. The last example above is less a splice issue than one of omitting the conjunction "but." Here are some justifiable examples, although a semicolon would avoid the criticism of comma splices. Use them with discretion.

This is my father, that is my uncle. They're twins.

That's not a sugar maple, it's a red maple.

The music ended, their dancing stopped. He looked into her expectant eyes and leaned closer. His lips touched hers. Mouths opened, tongues connected.

The breeze whispered softly and gently, tree branches danced and fell and made shadows on the earth and water.

I would pay her back, I would do anything to pay her back.

The sun was setting, the moon was rising. He had heard there would be a gale this morning, but they had sailed it out, and now the waves just rose and fell with a rhythmic beauty. The night was calm, the salt air was sweet, the breeze was cooling.

The last example has two comma splices: one in the first sentence and one at the end after "sweet." The second one is really a serial comma before the last element of a series where the "and" is omitted. This is a justifiable way to make the series stand out—but, again, use it sparingly.

[5.31] Misplaced & superfluous commas—ways to test

We can use the "most commas occur in pairs" principle to help detect misplaced or extra commas. By the rules we've given previously, phrases enclosed by commas should be nonessential and therefore removable. Without the phrase, the sentence should still make sense. Remember that the beginning and end of a sentence may "hide" a comma. Let's test this sentence:

Now, he wasn't sure if he was, imagining things that weren't there, or if things merely weren't as they should be.

First, remove "now" since it's followed by a comma and starts the sentence (the invisible comma of the pair).

He wasn't sure if he was, imagining things that weren't there, or if things merely weren't as they should be.

That works. Next, try removing "he wasn't sure if he was."

Now, imagining things that weren't there, or if things merely weren't as they should be.

Oops. It's an incomplete sentence. The comma after "was" is therefore incorrect. Delete it and continue.

Now, he wasn't sure if he was imagining things that weren't there, or if things merely weren't as they should be.

Remove the last phrase to test whether the comma after "there" belongs.

Now, he wasn't sure if he was imagining things that weren't there.

That works and we're done. Remove that one comma after "was" and we have a properly punctuated sentence. This technique isn't foolproof, but it will diagnose many comma problems. Here are some other examples with the superfluous—and incorrect—comma in brackets. Use the test to convince yourself that the comma is incorrect.

My wife[,] and I are planning a trip to Chicago next year.

Robert is the team captain[,] and the oldest guy on the team.

[5.32] Fine points of comma usage

Some of the examples in this section were borrowed (with permission) from Graeme Reynolds' werewolf novel *High Moor*. Comments follow the examples. Optional commas are shown in parentheses.

[5.32.1] Comma to differentiate word or phrase meaning

"As if" clauses perform different functions. In the example below, the first is a restrictive adverbial phrase describing the way her face sagged. The second "as if" clause is a parenthetical thought about why the voice was muted, hence we require a comma. Putting a comma before the first "as if" is not wrong, but it adds a pause that might be desirable in this context.

> Caroline Simpson looked tired. Her face had lost its colour, and her entire frame sagged(,) as if carrying an invisible load. She looked down at Marie, and(,) for a moment, said nothing. When she did speak, her voice was muted, as if the effort of speech was almost too much for her.

"Since" can mean "because" (a subordinating conjunction, with a comma), or "from some point in time" (an adverb, no comma). Both of the examples below are correct.

> Jacob slept in on Saturdays, since he didn't have to go to work.

> Jacob has slept in on Saturdays since he started staying out late on Friday nights.

"Then" as an adverb can mean "in that case," "at that time," or "next in sequence." We often see it used conjunctively by itself as in the second example below. Microsoft Word and some other grammar checkers flag it as an error and suggest "and then" to replace "then" when it's a conjunction.

> Show me then. (adverbial)

> Show me the results(,) then explain your logic.

Technically, the second example is a comma splice missing "and" before "then." Some authorities claim that "and then" is redundant because "then" provides a conjunctive link and shows a sequence of two events. We agree. At worst, "then" is a minor comma splice and therefore acceptable in fiction. We believe that "and then" gives the writing a stiffer feel, which is okay if that's what you desire.

[5.32.2] Comma changes the sentence meaning

A writer must be conscious of *how* a sentence reads compared to how it *should* read.

Most of the time travelers worry about their luggage. (We suspect that time travelers probably have more important things to worry about than their luggage.)

Most of the time, travelers worry about their luggage.

Steven's 4x4 was parked on the side of the street near to the trees. (One side of the street is near the trees, the other is not.)

Steven's 4x4 was parked on the side of the street, near to the trees. (It's parked nearer to the trees on that side as opposed to a spot on that same side farther from the trees.)

Yes, I'm sorry you did tell me your name. (You regret hearing the person's name?)

Yes, I'm sorry, you did tell me your name. (You forgot that the name was mentioned.)

Two clawed hands burst through the rotting wood to either side of Simon's head. (The wood is rotting on both sides of where his head is.)

Two clawed hands burst through the rotting wood, to either side of Simon's head. (This ignores the details of the rotting wood's location and focuses on the claws being next to his head.)

We kissed, and it tasted just as fresh and new as it did that very first time, at our wedding.

We kissed, and it tasted just as fresh and new as it did that very first time at our wedding.

These last two examples come from *Timecaster* by J. A. Konrath. In the first version (the way the author wrote it), the character is talking about the first kiss with his wife, period. In the second, the character may have kissed this woman before, but this is the first time they kissed at the wedding. The novel's context makes it clear why the distinction is significant.

And here is a classic example of punctuation changing meaning.

A woman without her man is nothing.

A woman: without her, man is nothing.

[5.32.3] Comma makes a subtle difference

I'll go and find him if you like.

I'll go and find him, if you like. (suggests more of a question in the voice)

For years he's slaughtered people like us all over the world.

For years he's slaughtered people like us, all over the world.

For years, he's slaughtered people like us, all over the world.

Marie edged towards the door. She felt a sudden need to be out of the house(,) before Mrs. Simpson started asking questions about where John might be or what he might be up to. (Note the difference in tone the comma makes after "house.")

His finger touched the trigger. Cold metal against warm skin. The finger curled around the trigger and tightened until he felt the pressure point. That final resistance before the weapon fired[,] and a young boy lay dead in the street. An elderly couple emerged from the house next to the telephone box and called to the boy.

To understand why the comma marked [,] in the last example is incorrect and should *not* be inserted here, we must examine the passage without the sentence fragments. The clause "a young boy lay dead in the street" seems to be an independent one joined to the previous one by "and." This is not the case here. It's a noun clause describing the result of going past the pressure point, after which the boy would be dead. Therefore, no comma should be used after "fired." Another way to write it makes the "that final resistance..." phrase an appositive to "pressure point."

His finger touched the trigger, cold metal against warm skin. The finger curled around the trigger and tightened until he felt the pressure point, that final resistance before the weapon fired and a young boy lay dead in the street. An elderly couple emerged from the house next to the telephone box and called to the boy.

CHAPTER SIX

SEMICOLON

[6.1] What is the semicolon?

Many people are confused about the use of the semicolon (;). Unlike the period and the comma that are the workhorses of sentence construction and can be used as much as required, four common pieces of punctuation exist to fine tune the flow of our sentences: semicolon, colon, dash, ellipsis. Because they are used for fine tuning, they should be used with care. As with exclamation marks, if overused, these marks may lose their effect.

Part of the confusion over the semicolon comes from whether it should be considered a relative of the period or of the comma. Being a period placed above a comma does suggest a schizophrenic nature, and its application over the years has not always been consistent. Its earliest use had it acting as a pause longer than a comma but shorter than a period, and some writers still see it that way.

> TIP: Treat the semicolon as a weak period, not a strong comma. Don't use it where you would not use a period, and don't use it to connect sentence fragments. (Exception: [6.5])

[6.2] Semicolon connecting closely related sentences

Traditionally, the semicolon has been used to connect two closely related sentences or independent clauses, replacing a period, but there are some restrictions.

Use a semicolon only when showing parallelism, contrast, or cause and effect.

[CORRECT]

Rebecca ordered a Coke. Jennifer ordered something stronger.

Rebecca ordered a Coke, but Jennifer ordered something stronger.

Rebecca ordered a Coke; Jennifer ordered something stronger. (contrast)

Ten years ago, Sam and I married our high school sweethearts. His marriage has survived; mine ended in a divorce. (contrast)

Jerry wears short sleeve shirts even in the winter; Evan wears them only in warm weather. (parallelism and contrast)

Pete came to the party sober; he was drunk an hour later. (cause and effect)

In most contracts, the large print giveth; the small print taketh away. (contrast)

He was twenty-one; he could buy beer. (cause and effect)

Do not capitalize the sentence or phrase following a semicolon unless it begins with a word that is normally capitalized.

Never use a semicolon to connect dependent clauses or fragments (not even if a period would be acceptable). Use a comma or another mark (or perhaps no punctuation at all). In some cases, you can use sentence fragments with a period but never with a semicolon. In the examples below, we've indicated possible choices to replace the incorrect semicolon, including using no punctuation (nothing).

[INCORRECT]

Neal likes quiet music in the background; when he is reading. (nothing)

Ellen likes ice skating; not roller skating. (comma)

I stayed up to finish my school project; all night long. (nothing, comma, dash)

Keep your friends close; Your enemies closer. (comma and no cap)

After he came in from shoveling snow, he sat in the chair; hugging himself; still shivering ten minutes later. (use commas to form a series or fragments with periods)

That night, Reese's life started on a downward spiral, although he didn't find out that it had; until a long while afterwards. (nothing, or a dash)

Darren had gone out with her four times and really liked her, but she didn't appear interested in pursuing the relationship; another failed attempt at romance. (dash or recast sentence)

He brought everything we needed for the bank job; guns, the ski masks, large satchels for the money. (colon)

It was raining this morning on the way to work; I really hate driving in the rain. (period, or comma and a conjunction)

The house's exterior showed years of neglect; the ivy growing over the windows. (poorly constructed, recast the sentences completely)

You should not use a semicolon to link two successive events that don't show parallelism, contrast, or cause and effect. In the examples below, the second sentence simply provides more information with no close parallelism. Either join them with a conjunction, or make them separate sentences.

[INCORRECT]

Eric finished his homework early; after that, he played video games until bedtime.

Carl arrived late; he also forgot to pick up the pizza.

We've seen the semicolon used in cases like these, the rationale being they're closely connected actions, but this risks overusing semicolons. (See [6.8]) Rely on periods and commas and reserve semicolons for when they're truly the best option.

[6.3] Tests for proper semicolon use

When considering whether a semicolon is appropriate, try two tests. First, substitute "but" or "and" between the two independent clauses. Is the result a good compound sentence? Second, do the elements being joined have a parallelism that makes them closely related? If you can answer yes to both questions, a semicolon is probably a viable choice.

[CORRECT—THESE PASS THE TESTS]

The tumblers of my mental lock turned; the combination fell into place.

If Jessica had looked angry before this, she was now furious. The red flecks in her brown eyes burned; her cheeks paled.

With me you have a chance; with him I guarantee you'll fail.

* * *

ADVANCED: SEMICOLON

[6.4] Semicolon connecting clauses with a conjunctive adverb

Conjunctive adverbs (e.g., however, therefore, nevertheless, instead—see [5.14] for a list) often signal a close connection between independent clauses. Therefore, a semicolon is appropriate to use before the conjunctive adverb. A comma usually follows it in these cases. When the connection between the conjunctive adverb and the clause following it is weak, the comma is optional.

NOTE: Some authorities may argue that some of the commas below are not optional and should be inserted.

I compute; therefore(,) I am.

They must have gotten wind of our planned attack and doubled up on the guards; nevertheless, we must proceed as planned if we hope to free the prisoners.

You can use semicolons in many places; however, that doesn't mean you should use them everywhere you can.

I had planned on going home; instead(,) I went to the bar.

These things really happened; otherwise(,) I wouldn't have claimed to have seen them.

[6.5] Semicolon to unclutter sentences with many commas

When writing a series where the individual items contain commas for other reasons, we can (and often should) use a semicolon in place of the commas that separate the items in the series. This makes the sentence visually less confusing. However, if a comma would be incorrect and the semicolon can't reasonably be replaced by a conjunction, then the semicolon is wrong. Consider how confusing the following sentences would be without the semicolons.

94

For dinner she served marinated, roast pork in a light orange sauce; cheese-topped, garlic mashed potatoes; coarsely chopped Brussels sprouts cooked with shallots and pancetta; and a divine, low-calorie orange-chocolate mousse for dessert.

The three men who currently had a claim on his life were all in the room: Dmitri Rostov, the Russian FSB agent; Stephen Hall, ex-Special Forces; and Joseph Angelo, mob boss.

Derek strode into the room wearing distressed, black jeans; brand-new, below-the-knee, black leather boots; a white, ruffled tuxedo shirt. His hands and wrists bore serious metal adornments: studded leather cuffs on each wrist; a jeweled, gold bracelet on his left wrist; and heavily engraved, silver rings on each thumb and ring finger.

Some say not to use a semicolon before "and" or "but" as in the last example, but see [6.8].

[6.6] Semicolons and simultaneous actions

Do not use a semicolon to connect two independent clauses that show *simultaneous* actions even if they seem closely related. This applies to clauses where "as" or "while" could be used.

[INCORRECT]

A sudden thundershower turned into a downpour; everyone at the outdoor reception was scrambling for shelter.

Susan finished packing for their trip; Harry did a final check of the house.

[CORRECT]

A sudden thundershower turned into a downpour, and everyone at the outdoor reception was scrambling for shelter.

While Susan finished packing for their trip, Harry did a final check of the house.

[6.7] Semicolons with sentence fragments

We've already discussed the merits of and cautions with using sentence fragments. Although we do advocate flexibility in

95

punctuation, that doesn't mean everything is allowed. Except for the use of semicolons in a series, do not use a semicolon where you would not use a period.

But this does *not* give you license to use a semicolon everywhere you would use a period. A semicolon has very specific uses, and those do not include it being a universal replacement for the period.

We can't think of a situation where it would be appropriate to use a semicolon with a sentence fragment. In chapter 1 we used three sentence variations of "She entered the room and stopped." None of those included a semicolon because the comma and the period accomplished the job. When using sentence fragments (sparingly), treat them as sentences by using a period.

[NO] All he ever wanted were happiness, a long life, and money; lots of it. (ugly sentence)

[YES] All he ever wanted were happiness, a long life, and money. Lots of it.

[YES] He only wanted three things: happiness, a long life—and money. Lots of it.

[NO] At the zoo he saw lions, and tigers; and no bears. (unjustified semicolon)

[YES] At the zoo he saw lions, and tigers. And no bears.

Don't confuse these examples with the "We argued; we begged..." ones below in [6.8]. Those are complete sentences (subject and verb), not fragments.

[6.8] Semicolons as stylistic options

Semicolons can be used to alter emphasis, but this should be a very rare use of them. Consider an analogy to "I came, I saw, I conquered."

We argued, we begged, we pleaded, and we lost the decision.

We argued. We begged. We pleaded. We lost the decision.

We argued, and we begged, and we pleaded, and we lost the decision.

We argued; we begged; we pleaded; we lost the decision.

We argued; we begged; we pleaded; and we lost the decision. (different emphasis from above despite violating the rule of no semicolon after "and")

In chapter 1 [1.6], we gave two famous quotes that used "inappropriate" semicolons.

"My father taught me to work; he did not teach me to love it." (Abraham Lincoln)

"Better we lose the election than mislead the people; and better we lose than misgovern the people." (Adlai Stevenson)

Lincoln's use is acceptable because there's a strong parallel in the statement. In Stevenson's, the ideas are also parallel. Without the semicolon and the conjunction, the sentence would not have the same flow and meaning.

NOTE: Do not overuse semicolons even if you are using them appropriately.

CHAPTER SEVEN

APOSTROPHE

[7.1] What is the apostrophe?

The apostrophe is both a spelling mark and grammar mark. In UK English it is sometimes called an inverted comma. It has two simple and well-defined functions, yet it causes a great deal of confusion to people who confuse plurals and possessives.

In the past, the apostrophe was used to form the plurals of numbers, letters, and some abbreviations. If you remember that you *never* use an apostrophe to make a word plural and learn the couple of logical exceptions that we'll mention in [7.8], you won't be confused.

[7.2] Apostrophe to show the omission of letters

[7.2.1] Apostrophes in contractions

In common contractions the apostrophe is used to show that two or more words have been contracted together and that one or more letters have been omitted in the process. Sometimes a single contraction has more than one meaning. This is also used for some numbers.

it's (it is—not to be confused with "its" [see 7.3.2.1])

isn't (is not)

aren't (are not)

wouldn't (would not)

won't (will not)

could've (could have)

we'd (we had, we would)

she'll (she will)

I'd've / he'd've (I/he would have—rare contraction)

there's (there is, there has)

who's (who is—not to be confused with "whose" [see 7.3.2.2])

you're (you are)

o'clock (of the clock)

the class of '73. (1973)

I remember the '60s all too well. (1960s—older usage had an apostrophe: 1960's)

[7.2.2] Apostrophes to show dialect

By extension of their use in contractions, apostrophes are used to show the omission of letters in speech when writing certain dialects or casual speech.

TIP: While the use of dialect in writing can add flavor to the speech of your characters, reading it may be difficult. Use dialect with care. Consider these examples.

He ain't goin' to town with me. (acceptable)

If'n you ain't eatin' proper, ya'll be gettin' sick. (acceptable)

He ain't comin' 'cause he gots plowin' ta do 'fore th' firs' snow come. (difficult to read)

She won' be com'n' 'long wi' me t' th' meetin'. (very difficult)

[7.3] Apostrophe to show possession

A possessive is grammatically called a *genitive*. This means that it shows possession, ownership, or origin. All possessives are genitives, but the reverse if not true. With only one exception (possessive pronouns [7.3.2]), all genitives require an apostrophe.

Maggie's horse is two years old. (genitive and possessive—the horse belongs to Maggie)

The men's room (genitive, not possessive—it doesn't belong to the men)

A year's wages (genitive, not possessive)

A girls' school (genitive, not possessive—the girls don't own the school)

99

She put her children's books back on the shelf. (genitive and possessive—the books belong to the children.)

She writes children's books. (genitive, not possessive—these books do not belong to children.)

[7.3.1] Forming the possessive (or genitive)

In English, a possessive is normally formed by adding an apostrophe to the end of the *singular* noun, followed by the letter *s* ('s). This rule works for proper nouns, numbers, and names ending in *s*, *x*, or *z*. Some historical names used to be exceptions (See sections [7.6.1] and [7.6.2])

To form the possessive of a *plural* noun ending in *s*, add a simple apostrophe to the end of the noun.

If the word is an *irregular plural*, one not ending in *s* (e.g., men, women, children), add 's to the plural form.

The dog's bone (the bone belonging to the dog)

The library's books (the books belonging to the library)

All of the libraries' books in our town are catalogued online. (the books in several libraries)

The destruction of the World Trade Towers was 2001's most tragic event. (event belonging to that year)

A woman's rights (the rights of one woman)

Women's rights (the rights of more than one woman)

The werewolf's teeth were bared. (one werewolf)

The werewolves' teeth were bared. (more than one werewolf)

My friend's parents went to the game with us. (the parents of one friend)

All of my friends' parents showed up at the rally. (the parents of all your friends showed up)

My son's friends' parents all attended his graduation ceremony. (one son, several friends)

[7.3.2] Possessive pronouns never take an apostrophe

The possessive pronouns (mine, yours, his, hers, its, ours, theirs, whose) *never* take an apostrophe. This is the source of confusion between "it's" and "its."

Your car is newer than her car. (Yours is newer than hers.)

Our house is older than their house. (Ours is older than theirs.)

[7.3.2.1] It's and its

"Its" is the possessive pronoun (meaning belonging to "it").

The cat's toys are all chewed up. Its toys are all chewed up.

"It's" is the contraction for "it is."

NOTE: Do *not* rely on grammar checkers to catch errors with these.

To test for which one to use, substitute "it is." If the sentence makes sense, then "it's" is correct. Otherwise, use "its."

[CORRECT] That car sounds really loud. It's possible that its muffler has a hole in it or else one of its exhaust pipes is loose.

[TEST] That car sounds really loud. (It is) possible that (it is) muffler has a hole in it or else one of (it is) exhaust pipes is loose.

Since only the first "it is" substitution makes sense, that one takes the contraction "it's." The other two should be "its."

[7.3.2.2] Who's and whose

"Who's" is the contraction of "who is." "Whose" is the possessive pronoun.

Whose car are we taking? (Who does the car belong to)

Who's going with us? (Who is going with us?)

I don't care who's going or whose car we take.

Test the same way we did for "it's/its" by substituting "who is."

[TEST] I don't care (who is) going or (who is) car we take.

Only the first substitution makes sense. Use "who's" for that one and "whose" for the other.

[7.4] Apostrophe changes the meaning of some words

its, it's
ill, I'll
wont, won't
cant, can't

NOTE: Readers unfamiliar with the meanings of "wont" and "cant" should look those up.

INTERESTING SIDE NOTE: In his novel *As I Lay Dying*, William Faulkner curiously uses "cant" and "wont" for "can't" and "won't" yet he uses other standard contractions with the apostrophe.

TIP 1: A possessive will *always* have an apostrophe (except possessive pronouns).

TIP 2: A simple plural (rare exceptions) will *never* have an apostrophe.

* * *

ADVANCED: APOSTROPHE

[7.5] Plurals of nouns with postpositive adjectives

Figuring out the plurals of some nouns can make your hair hurt. In-laws can be a headache, a good reason to avoid in-laws in your fiction. It's best to look up such unconventional plurals to be sure you've written them correctly.

One son-in-law

Two sons-in-law

My son-in-law's new wife (one son-in-law)

My two sons-in-law's new wives (both sons-in-law have new wives)

My two sons-in-law's new wives' cars (the new cars that belong to the new wives of both your sons-in-law)

In nouns such as these, because the adjective follows the noun it describes, the term "postpositive adjective" is used. Here are some other nouns using postpositive adjectives.

postmaster general, secretary general, attorney general, notary public, editor in chief, right-of-way, sergeant-at-arms, court-martial, heir apparent.

Once you recognize the situation, it's easy to figure out how to form their plurals. You make the *noun* part plural: attorneys general, editors in chief, rights-of-way, courts-martial, etc.

[7.6] Possessives of names ending in "s"

How should one show possession when a person's name ends in *s*? The 16th edition of the CMOS recommends the *'s* instead of just the apostrophe, but both ways are acceptable. Whichever style you choose, be consistent. You have a character named Cyrus Hayes and he has henchmen. Therefore—

Cyrus's henchmen (preferred), or Cyrus' henchmen.

Cyrus Hayes's henchmen (preferred), or Cyrus Hayes' henchmen

[7.6.1] Possessive forms of certain historical names

Certain historical names used to be special cases, but the CMOS now recommends adding the *'s* to them: *Achilles, Ganges, Jesus, Moses, Xerxes* become *Jesus's, Moses's*, etc.

These had a longstanding convention of using just the apostrophe, and many sources still list them that way (Jesus', Moses' Euripides', Isis'). This was based on the idea that names ending with an *ez* or *iz* would be awkward pronounced with the added *'s* sound. You still pronounce *Moses's commandments* and *Moses' commandments* the same, as if the extra *s* were absent.

[7.6.2] Possessives of words ending in silent "s"

The CMOS forms these possessives with *'s* for consistency.

Descartes's contributions to mathematics

The marquis's estate

Albert Camus's novels

[7.7] Singular/plural possessive confusion

Sometimes you're not sure whether to use the possessive singular or possessive plural or even what the possessive plural should be.

It was the people's decision to make.

At the gathering of the clans, the various peoples' wishes were made clear.

"People" has two different meanings in these sentences. The first is the plural of "person." As with all words that have irregular plurals (e.g., children, women), add 's: people's.

The second meaning is a singular word referring to one group (a race, clan, nationality). The plural of that word is "peoples." Form the possessive by adding only an apostrophe: peoples'.

Confusion also arises when a word is the same in the singular and plural (e.g., deer). The context must specify whether the word is singular or plural. *Deers'* is never a correct form.

We followed the deer's tracks easily after the buck entered the snowy woods. (one deer)

We followed the deer's tracks easily after the animals crossed the snowy field. (more than one deer)

Sometimes we're not sure which form to use.

As soon as he arrived at the hospital, Rob went to the nurse's/nurses' desk to ask which room his brother was in.

Which version do we use? Does the station refer to a place where one nurse or several nurses might be found? If it's a small facility and only one nurse is around, use *nurse's*. If multiple nurses are present use *nurses'*.

Do we refer to a *writers handbook, writer's handbook,* or *writers' handbook*? We've seen them all used. In the first, "writers" is a simple adjective: a book for writers in a generic sense. A writer's handbook suggests it is for the individual, a more personal designation. A "writers' handbook" conveys this same thing for multiple individuals.

[7.8] Plurals with apostrophes—exceptions

[7.8.1] Plurals of numerals and abbreviations

An older practice used the apostrophe with these (1960's, CD's, PhD's), an exception to apostrophes with plurals. Current standard practice is *not* to use an apostrophe in dates or numbers or in abbreviations using capital letters. The following are correct.

I remember the 1960s like they were yesterday.

Six of the employees in the company hold PhDs, and nine more hold MAs.

The CEOs of seven companies attended the convention.

How many CDs do you own?

[7.8.2] Plurals of letters

The CMOS recommends not using an apostrophe with the plural of capital letters unless confusion would result without the apostrophe. The following are correct.

We learned the three Rs in school.

On her report card she received all As and Bs this semester.

Lowercase letters use the apostrophe to avoid confusion with another word or abbreviation.

x's and y's

Be sure to dot your i's and cross your t's. (not "is" and "ts")

Mind your p's and q's.

Bob Babbitt has a lot of b's in his name. ("bs" would be confusing and amusing)

There are two a's in "manual." (the alternative "as" would be viewed as a typographical error)

When one plural letter in the sentence needs an apostrophe, but others don't, be consistent and use apostrophes for all.

"Accommodate" contains two a's, two c's, and two m's.

[7.9] Non-obvious plural forms

Note that the following do not use apostrophes for the plural.

ifs and buts

thank-yous

maybes

yeses and nos

dos and don'ts (some writers prefer "do's" for clarity.)

Yes-men respond with yeses, never contemplate noes, but maybe consider maybes in moments of indecision.

[7.10] Compound possession

[7.10.1] Compound possession with nouns

When you have two or more joint owners of something, only the last noun takes the possessive.

John and Mary's car is parked in the garage. (car belongs to both of them)

John and Mary's two cars are parked in the garage. (cars belong to both of them)

Steve and Wendy's vacation is booked in June. (they're going on a vacation together)

Tyler, Jeff, and Sam's toys are scattered all over the place. (the toys belong to all three.)

When the items are separately owned, all of the nouns take the possessive.

John's and Mary's cars are both parked in the garage. (they each own a car)

Alan's and Carol's clothes are packed for their trip. (they have separate clothes—unless they share clothes and wear the same size)

Steve's and Wendy's vacations are booked in June. (they're going on separate vacations)

When you're not sure if your reader will interpret it correctly, reword the sentence.

Steve and Wendy both have their vacations in June.

Steve and Wendy have booked a vacation together in June.

John and Mary park their cars on the street.

[7.10.2] Compound possession with pronouns

When a noun and possessive pronoun are involved, the noun must be possessive, but *never* add 's to a pronoun to make it possessive. In many of these cases, it is better to reword the sentence to avoid confusion or awkwardness.

[INCORRECT]

Jenny's and my's cat snuck out of the house.

My brother and I's apartment was robbed yesterday.

Craig's and her's toys were scattered around the room.

[CORRECT]

Jenny's and my cat snuck out of the house (one cat, belongs to both)

Jenny's and my cats snuck out of the house. (one or more cats belonging to each person separately)

Jenny's cat and my cat both snuck out of the house. (clearer)

My brother's and my apartment was robbed yesterday.

The apartment where my brother and I live was robbed yesterday. (clearer)

Craig's and her toys were scattered around the room.

[7.11] Miscellaneous possessives issues

You want to make "a friend of me and my sister got married yesterday" into a possessive.

[INCORRECT] Me and my sister's friend got married yesterday.

This might be okay in dialogue if that's how your character talks, but it's bad grammar and ambiguous. Did you *and* your sister's friend get married separately, or did you marry your sister's friend? Reword for clarity.

My sister's friend and I got married yesterday, but not to each other.

I married my sister's friend yesterday.

[INCORRECT] A friend of my brother's stopped by my house today.

The "of my brother" is already a possessive form. The 's on "brother" is redundant as well as incorrect.

[CORRECT] A friend of my brother stopped by my house today.

CHAPTER EIGHT

HYPHEN

[8.1] What is the hyphen?

The hyphen is made by pressing the minus key on either the main keyboard or on the numeric keypad, if you have one.

The hyphen, like the apostrophe, is a grammatical and spelling mark that serves both joining and separating functions. Do not put spaces before or after a hyphen. (But see [10.5])

[8.2] Hyphen for formatting lines on the page

In print books, words may be hyphenated at the end of lines, between syllables, in order to make the text even on the right-hand side of the page. In e-books, which have variable page and font sizes, the hyphenation of words does not serve well for this purpose and will mess up the formatting. This would be addressed in the final formatting stage for print books, not in the writing stage.

[8.3] Basic uses of hyphens

[8.3.1] Hyphens in telephone numbers

The caller ID showed the incoming number as 716-555-1234.

[8.3.2] Hyphens in certain addresses

She lives at 233-5 Main Street, Smalltown, NC.

[8.3.3] Hyphen as part of the spelling of certain words
brother-in-law
co-op
H-bomb
make-believe
T-shirt
U-turn
x-ray

[8.3.4] Hyphens with certain prefixes

self-control
ex-girlfriend
mid-July (before a proper noun)
re-cover (to differentiate it from "recover")
semi-industrial (to avoid double letter "i" together)

See [8.9] for further details on prefixes.

[8.3.5] Compound adjectives and phrases as a single adjective

Air Force brats got rides in high-tech planes, but we Army brats got stuck in low-tech jeeps.

Across the flowing, debris-free, mud-free river we saw canoes docked.

He slouched to make his six-foot-three, broad-shouldered frame less inconspicuous.

Last night we dined at an all-you-can-eat buffet.

His chin sported a shaved-last-night stubble.

The pilot made a sharp bank-and-turn maneuver.

[8.3.6] Hyphens to show a word being spelled out

"I said *no*, not *yes*! What part of n-o sounds like y-e-s?"

My last name is "Gamboe" not "Gamble": G-A-M-B-O-E.

Rough, *cough*, and *though* all end in o-u-g-h, but that letter combination is pronounced differently in each one.

[8.3.7] Hyphens to indicate stuttering speech

His hands shook as he spoke. "I d-don't th-think I c-c-can d-do this." (See [8.13])

[8.3.8] Hyphens to show speech dialects

"I'm a-thinkin' I should be a-leavin' about now."

[8.3.9] Hyphenate the numbers from 21 to 99

The numbers 21-99 and round numbers (a hundred, thousand, million) should be spelled out unless it's awkward to do so. Larger numbers that are not round values are usually written as numerals, but they can be spelled out for emphasis.

Years are usually written as numerals.

NOTE: *Never* start a sentence with numerals. Rewrite the sentence to avoid this.

[CORRECT]

The town's population is 3,527.

We're proud of our little town, all three-thousand, five-hundred, and twenty-seven of us! (While the hyphen is normally used only for the 27, for consistency, and emphasis, add hyphens in the other numbers in cases like this.)

We agreed on $1500, not $2000.

We agreed on fifteen hundred dollars, not two thousand.

We agreed on one-thousand(,) five-hundred dollars(,) not two thousand. (comma optional for extra emphasis only because the hyphens for emphasis already make the division clear)

[INCORRECT]

1982 is the year I was born.

$50,000 is what we agreed on for the job.

6 steaks should be enough for the barbecue.

[8.3.10] For number ranges, one *may* use a hyphen

Technically, the en-dash, not a hyphen, should be used with number ranges. (See [8.6])

I have attached pages 16-20 of the relevant document. (hyphen)

I have attached pages 16–20 of the relevant document. (en-dash, preferred)

[8.4] When to hyphenate specific words

There is no simple set of rules in English as to which words get hyphenated. Worse, the language is always changing. It's always wise to check a current dictionary even when you think you know. Some prefixes and suffixes that used to be hyphenated all the time now rarely are, but exceptions still exist. The CMOS has an extensive section on compound words by category, and in [8.9] we cover the more important ones.

[8.5] Compound adjectives

When two or more words are used as a single adjective, put hyphens between *all* of the adjectives when they precede the noun, but usually not when they follow it.

He hates getting up in the early morning.

He hates an early-morning class even more.

I studied for a half hour last night.

Some TV sitcoms are half-hour programs.

He is well read.

He is a well-read person.

His day started out not so great.

He had a not-so-great start to his day.

This airline does not serve meals in flight.

Some airlines serve in-flight meals.

My neighbor across the street has a daughter who is seven years old.

My neighbor across the street has a seven-year-old daughter.

As we approached the town, a premonition slithered underneath my being-watched feeling.

His unwise actions put him first on their to-do list.

By convention, don't hyphenate "ly" adverbs in descriptions. Hyphenate *only* the adjectives, not the nouns. (See [8.7])

[INCORRECT]

It was a beautifully-written poem. (no hyphen)

My fear is that they'll strap me to a chair, aim nasty bright lights at me, and inject me with turn-your-brain-to-mush-drugs. ("drugs" is a noun, not an adjective—no hyphen after "mush")

My neighbor across the street has a seven-year-old-daughter. ("daughter" is not an adjective—no hyphen after "old")

* * *

ADVANCED: HYPHEN

[8.6] En-dash for number ranges

Many people, unaware of the en-dash's existence, will use the hyphen with number ranges. We doubt that most fiction readers will know or care, and in some fonts the difference from the hyphen is hardly noticeable. In other fonts (like Times New Roman), the difference is readily apparent. Unless you're picky, using a hyphen will save you having to remember when to use the en-dash.

Refer to chapter 10 for details on the en-dash and how to enter it. The examples below use the en-dash correctly.

The convention will be held July 25–July 27, 2014.

Please read pages 45–66 for tomorrow.

Albert Einstein (1879–1955) was a theoretical physicist.

Our team beat theirs, 21–20.

Tomorrow night the band will play 8 P.M.–1 A.M.

NOTE: In number ranges, the en-dash replaces the word "to." Therefore, do not use the en-dash (or hyphen) if "to" or "from...to" is used.

John F. Kennedy served as President of the U.S. from 1961 to 1963.

Tonight the band will play from 7:00 to 11:00.

[8.7] Compound adjectives

[8.7.1] Which words to hyphenate in compounds

Hyphenate all of the adjectives and *only* the adjectives, not the nouns with them. This is easy to figure out if you look at what is being described. Look at the noun, then look at the words describing it. Consider the following hyphenation problems and their solutions.

[CONFUSING] The storm caused two hour long delays for most flights. (How many delays and how long were they?)

[GOOD] The storm caused two, hour-long delays. (2 delays of 1 hour each)

[GOOD] The storm caused two-hour-long delays. (multiple delays, each 2 hours long)

[CONFUSING] The driver sustained non-life threatening injuries in the crash. (The driver had non-life injuries that were threatening?)

[GOOD] The driver sustained non-life-threatening injuries in the crash.

[CONFUSING] Our team broke its ten-year-old-team record of six home runs in a single game. (This says the team is ten years old and broke the record among teams that were ten years old as well, which doesn't make sense.)

[GOOD] Our team broke its ten-year-old team record of six home runs in a single game.

Hyphenation can change the meaning of the sentence.

"A man-eating shark" is a shark that eats humans, but "A man eating shark" is a human eating shark meat.

A dirty magazine rack might turn some customers away, but a dirty-magazine rack might attract them.

[8.7.2] Descriptive phrases as adjectives

When using a descriptive phrase, hyphenate the parts of it only when it's before the noun.

I hate him and his wheeling-and-dealing ways.

He does a lot of wheeling and dealing.

Take a wait-and-see attitude.

We will wait and see what happens next.

We provided an up-to-date solution.

Keep your computer's antivirus software up to date.

His mother gave him a don't-even-think-about-it look.

When the phrase is a longer one, putting it in quotes creates a better appearance. We discuss this further in chapter 12.

His mother gave him a "don't even think about it" look.

[8.7.3] Words ending in "ly"

Do not hyphenate "ly" adverbs (because they're not adjectives). In chapter 2 we pointed out some "ly" words that *are* adjectives. Those should be hyphenated in compound adjectives.

a really beautiful woman (adverb, no hyphen)

a silly-looking hat (adjective)

a beautifully crafted sculpture (adverb)

a highly flammable liquid (adverb)

an unusually friendly-seeming person (*friendly* is an adjective; *unusually* is an adverb)

How can you tell if an "ly" word is an adjective or an adverb? Easy. Simply put the "ly" word alone with a noun and see if it makes sense. If it does, then it's an adjective. In the examples below, we've indicated which are adjectives and which are adverbs.

a really woman (adverb)

a silly hat (adjective)

a highly liquid (adverb)

a friendly person (adjective)

an unusually person (adverb)

a beautifully sculpture (adverb)

[8.7.4] Test for adjective hyphenation

This separation technique can also be used to tell if the adjectives should be hyphenated at all. If the adjective closest to the noun does *not* make sense alone with the noun but the adjectives together make sense, then hyphenation is necessary. All of the examples below do *not* make sense separated. Therefore, hyphenate.

a heavenly meal, a tasting meal (heavenly-tasting)

a friendly person, a seeming person (friendly-seeming)

a silly hat, a looking hat (silly-looking)

We belabor this point because some writers fail to hyphenate compound adjectives in the first place, which yields sloppy writing.

[INCORRECT]

No one paid attention to the middle aged man seated on the bench. ("aged man" makes sense alone, but he's a middle-aged man, not an aged man seated in the middle)

A twenty-foot tall steel fence surrounded the encampment. (twenty-foot-tall)

In this last example, we don't hyphenate *steel* because it's a separate adjective. "Twenty-foot-tall" describes the height, while "steel" describes the material. "A twenty-foot tall steel fence" is a tall fence that is twenty feet long and made of steel, and we'd need a comma after "foot" in that case: a twenty-foot, tall steel fence.

[8.7.5] Multi-word colors

Compound colors, such as blue-green, red-orange, as well as referring to light and dark colors, can cause problems.

yellow green eyed cat (yellow, green-eyed cat vs. yellow-green-eyed cat)

We usually don't hyphenate *dark* or *light* when referring to the depth of color unless there is an ambiguity. *Dark* has only one meaning, but *light* can also mean light in weight.

If we say a person has dark blue eyes or dark brown hair, there's no confusion, but what about a dark yellow room? Is the room painted a dark yellow, or is it a yellow room that's not well lit? In such a case, you would be better off rewording the sentence.

bright green and red peppers (Are both colors bright or only the green ones? Do we mean "bright-green and red peppers" or "bright, green and red peppers"?)

a bright green and red dress (Here we have an additional choice. Unlike the peppers, the dress can also be two colors: a bright, green-and-red dress")

We previously discussed how commas can sometimes mean "and" in sentences and how to use that when testing a series of adjectives for needed commas.

a dark brown suit (a suit that has a dark brown color)

a light, brown suit (a suit that is lightweight and brown, but better to reword as "a lightweight, brown suit))

bright blue eyes (the color is bright blue)

bright, blue eyes (eyes that are bright independent of color)

It's not always necessary to make these distinctions, but be aware of possible misreading.

"He was driving a mint green car" has two possible meanings.

He was driving a mint-green car. (color is mint green)

He was driving a mint, green car. (where "mint" is slang for "new," "cool," or "awesome")

He was driving a mint, mint-green car.

[8.8] Compound nouns

The English language is often a mess of contradictions. Is a particular term two words, one word, or hyphenated? Compound words are referred to in three ways: open (the words are separated), closed (one word), or hyphenated. A form that used to be open or hyphenated and is now one word is called a "permanent compound" (*sweat shirt* went to *sweat-shirt* then to *sweatshirt*).

TIP: *Never* trust spell checkers to get these right. Always look them up.

While there are no rules here, one piece of advice helps. When a noun or verb has two or more parts that convey one idea, it will often be a closed compound or hyphenated—but still look it up because the language is rapidly changing. Further, some words are open as nouns but hyphenated as adjectives or verbs. The following lists will demonstrate the problems.

quarterback, quarterstaff, quartermaster, quarter horse, quarter note

basketball, racquetball, tennis ball; rail fence, railroad; rain check, raincoat; bathroom, dining room; breakup, break-in; cross section, cross-reference, crossbow; schoolhouse, courthouse, safe house; vice president, vice-chancellor; stepfather, step stool; brand-new, brand name (noun), brand-name (adjective); high school; name-dropping; handwriting; fine-tune; color code (noun), color-code (verb)

Some words are the same for both the noun and verb forms: double-click, upgrade, downgrade, bullshit (but two words when referring to the actual excrement of a bull: bull shit).

Consider the following examples.

Takeout usually refers to fast food that you take out from a fast-food restaurant.

"About face!" screamed the sergeant for the troops to execute an about-face.

Two people break up then make up after the breakup.

A make-up artist applies makeup (or make-up).

You spray paint from a can in order to spray-paint graffiti on a wall.

When you hand off the football to a teammate, it's a hand-off.

Turn the lights out when it's time for lights-out.

When I screw up, my screw-ups are epic.

Some writers like to use brand names (noun) when their characters are wearing brand-name (adjective) clothing.

He writes science fiction (noun), therefore he is a science-fiction (adjective) writer.

Technological terms used in a technological context may be closed but open in other contexts: home page, homepage; file name, filename; voice mail, voicemail. And we have email or e-mail, depending on the user's preference. In these cases, the writer can decide which to use based on the context, but he should be consistent throughout a given work.

[8.9] Hyphenation of prefixes & suffixes

When it comes to prefixes and suffixes, the rules vary. The CMOS has an extensive set of tables for most of the prefixes and suffixes you'll encounter. We've listed the more common ones here. For these, "open" means hyphenated and "closed" means one word.

[8.9.1] Common prefixes generally not hyphenated

ANTI, BI, CO, DE; MEGA, MICRO, MID, MINI, NON, OVER, POST, PRE, PRO, RE, SEMI, SUB, UN, UNDER (antihero, bisexual, cooperate, megavitamin, microeconomics, midthirties, minivan, nonexistent, overexcited, posttraumatic, prewar, proindustrial, redo, unemployed, underachiever)

Hyphenate to avoid doubling a vowel (anti-inflammatory, anti-art, co-op, de-emphasize, mega-annoyance) and when a proper noun follows (pre-Columbian, mid-June, un-American, post-World War II).

BUT: mid-1990s, non-beer-drinking, pro-life, preempt

[8.9.2] The prefixes EX- and SELF- are usually hyphenated

ex-partner, ex-assassin, self-destructive, self-employed, self-conscious, self-restraint (but selfless, unselfconscious)

[8.9.3] Suffixes -LIKE and -NESS are almost never hyphenated

The default is to omit the hyphen with these two suffixes, but note these exceptions and examples.

(1) Hyphenate when a triple-ell (or triple-en) would result with the suffix: shell-like.

(2) The AP style guide prefers to hyphenate when the root word is three or more syllables (emulsion-like).

(3) Hyphenate when or the root word is a proper noun (Apple-like computer).

(4) Some like to hyphenate when the word ends in a vowel (cheese-like, maze-like), but "lifelike" is an exception to that.

(5) Use an optional hyphen to stress the suffix.

(6) Optionally hyphenate to avoid confusion or when the word might appear strange or awkward without the hyphen (elflike, weasellike).

> He was a fortyish, weasel-like, balding man in a business suit.

> There was a strangeness about him, an alien-ness, that Troy couldn't put his finger on.

> Jonathan could tell it was an inn and not just a tavern. It had more inn-ness than tavern-ness to it.

> Jake reminded me of my late-eighties TV hero, MacGyver. I saw definite MacGyver-ness in the way Jake used whatever was on hand to do what needed to be done.

> I said he was vampire-*like*, not a vampire.

[8.9.4] Suffix -ISH

The CMOS does not cover the "ish" suffix. Hundreds of English words incorporate it naturally without a hyphen (reddish, bluish, brownish, childish, bookish). The problem comes when you use a word with that prefix that likely wouldn't be in the dictionary or that looks strange even if correct. For example, *fivish*, *fiveish*, and *tennish* are all in the dictionary, but more than a few readers would likely question them.

We suggest the hyphen, especially if you want to stress the suffix. If a writer wishes to use "ish" with the hyphen as a stylistic effect, we see nothing wrong with it.

> He interrupted my Zen-ish moment to ask me a stupid question.

> As soon as I walked into Ken's apartment, his overly friendly, mini-ish schnauzer greeted me. (Here you also avoid the doubled vowel.)

> He found it a challenge balancing his new job duties with the required-ish social events that seemed to go along with it.

Always hyphenate "ish" with numbers, such as dates.

> The house was done in 1950-ish decor.

[8.10] Specific hyphenation notes

[8.10.1] Age terms: Hyphenate both nouns and adjectives

> He is a four-year-old boy.

> A group of four-year-olds were playing on the sidewalk.

[8.10.2] Colors: Hyphenate before the noun but not after

> She wore a snow-white dress.

> Her dress was snow white.

[8.10.3] Compass points

Compass points are closed as two directions, hyphenated if three or if "from...to" is implied)

> northeast

> west-northwest

> The street runs north-south. (from north to south)

[8.10.4] Family relationships

GREAT- and -IN-LAW are hyphenated; GRAND and STEP are closed

> grandfather; great-grandfather; great-great-grandmother; grand-uncle; grand-niece (The CMOS prefers *grand uncle* and *grand niece* open, with no hyphen); brother-in-law; parents-in-law; stepson; stepsister; stepparent (but *step-grandson* and *step-great-grandson*)

> NOTE: Some references show non-parental relationships as hyphenated. MS Word oddly accepts *grand uncle* as open but wants *grandniece* closed.

[8.10.5] Foreign phrases

Foreign phrases are open unless the original is hyphenated.

> in vitro fertilization

[8.10.6] Fractions and compounds

> a half hour (half-hour in some dictionaries)

> a half-hour appointment

> two-thirds of a cup; a two-thirds majority

> a one twenty-fifth share

> a quarter mile

> a half-kilometer race

[8.10.7] "Half" words

Since *half-* words are very common, we'll give them special mention. The CMOS says that adjective forms are always hyphenated before and after the noun and that noun forms are open (with some exceptions). But there are a *lot* of noun exceptions.

> halfback, halfcocked, halfhearted, halfway

> half-asleep, half-assed, half-breed, half-life (n and adj), half-light, half-mast, half-moon, half-pint, half-truth

half blood (or half-blood), a half hour (or half-hour), half note, half sister, half smile

NOTE: MS Word flags "half brother" and "half sister" as wrong but accepts them as hyphenated. They are open compounds.

[8.10.8] Numbers with nouns and abbreviations

a 10 cm diameter (no hyphen with abbreviations)

a 5 ft. high wall

a 40-page book

four inches high

a two-and-a-half-foot high wall

two and half feet

a six-foot-three basketball player

her twenty-third year in this job

He's six foot three.

a fourth-floor apartment

a spectacular 58th-floor view of the city

[8.10.9] Percentages

Percentages are always open as nouns or adjectives. The CMOS prefers using the word "percent" instead of the % sign and using numerals with percentages unless they begin a sentence.

The discount is 50 percent.

The CEO received a 50 percent raise last year.

Ten percent of the profits is the least I will accept.

[8.10.10] Proper nouns

Proper nouns are always open unless "between" is implied (*) or the first word is a prefix (**).

an Italian American

African American president

the South Central region

Middle Eastern countries

*the Franco-Prussian War

*the US-Canada border

**Anglo-Americans

[8.10.11] Time

Time references are usually open unless used as an adjective.

> The flight arrives at four thirty.

> He took a four-thirty flight.

> The four o'clock bus (an adjective, but an exception because of the "o'clock")

> The 6:00 p.m. news (don't hyphenate with numerals)

[8.11] Hyphenate to avoid confusion with another word

> You *recover* from an illness, but you *re-cover* a sleeping child whose blanket has come off.

> You *relay* a message, but you *re-lay* broken floor tiles.

> After the landlord *released* John from his rental agreement, he *re-leased* the apartment.

> I enjoy painting as a form of *recreation*, and my current project is to do a *re-creation* of the Mona Lisa.

> You resign from a job, but you re-sign a changed contract.

[8.12] Hyphens in a tmesis

A *tmesis* (pronounced "tuh-MEE-sis") is the separation of the parts of a compound word by another word or phrase. Hyphens (not dashes) surround the inserted word or phrase.

Abso-bloody-lutely

un-freaking-believable

The grammatically incorrect expression "a whole nother thing" is an example of a tmesis. If you need to use it in your writing, add hyphens: "a-whole-nother thing."

A few English words have absorbed a tmesis: whatsoever, whosoever, howsoever, etc.

[8.13] Hyphens with stuttered speech

When using the hyphen for stuttered speech, pay attention to where the hyphens break the words so that you retain the proper stuttered sound. Words that start with a *t* will be treated differently depending on what letter follows. The following example shows attention to the *sounds*, not the letters.

> T-t-trust me. R-reading m-minds i-is diff-i-i-c-cult. Y-you c-can't al-always t-tell for sh-sure wh-what some-wh-one is th-thinking a-b-bout.

This is an extreme example of stuttered speech and should be used to this extent only rarely. You can usually show stuttered or nervous speech with a lighter application of this technique. Someone this nervous probably won't be speaking much and probably not in long sentences. How those around this character react might give you a valid reason to limit this type of speech.

[8.14] Miscellaneous notes on hyphens and compounds

Some prefer *co-worker* to *coworker* so the eye sees *co-* and not *cow*. Either is correct.

With new words rapidly entering our language, it can be hard to find a consistent spelling until the word "settles in." E-mail or email? Cell phone, cell-phone, cellphone? Big screen TV, big-screen TV, bigscreen TV? You'll see all of these on the Internet, and dictionaries may not agree. (The term "bigscreen TV" is giving way to HDTV, which nicely solves the problem.)

We're allowed a bit of freedom as writers as long as it makes sense, we're consistent, and it doesn't violate long-time practice. In her novel *To Kill a Mockingbird*, written in the early 1960s, author Harper Lee uses *livingroom* as one word. She does it consistently, although we have no idea why she did this or why the publisher left it that way.

We can use hyphens as a flexible and creative tool.

> On the other hand, Dev Antos wasn't behaving like what I expected a mayor to behave like. He seemed... Dev-ious, and he had admitted to a clandestine past. (wordplay on his Dev's name)

=====

> The alien honchos regarded each other as if not expecting us to speak their language.
> "Purpose journey-stream home-place cross?" one asked.
> Colorful language. Or maybe my translator battery was running low.
> Kedda indicated our destination. "Journey-end. Night stay, nourish rest, provision buy."

=====

> The bartender's furtive look sent the cold pricklies to search-and-destroy the surviving warm fuzzies inside me.

NOTE: "Search and destroy" as a compound verb would normally not be hyphenated. One would normally hyphenate it only as a noun or adjective: "The team went on a search-and-destroy mission" or "The team went on a search-and-destroy." The discretionary hyphenation of the verbs in the example emphasizes a single-action verb phrase.

CHAPTER NINE

COLON

[9.1] Introduction to the colon

The colon has two basic functions: to introduce, and to separate. It has specific purposes and should not be used as a replacement for any other piece of punctuation. When we discuss the dash (em-dash), we'll see that writers sometimes confuse its uses with those of the colon, and we'll show you how to tell which is the better choice. Do not overuse the colon. Make sure it's your best option.

[9.2] Colon conventions

Before we detail the colon's use, we will explain the conventions of its use first.

[9.2.1] Spacing around a colon

Put a single space after a colon but no space before it.

EXCEPTIONS: When designating time, (in either 12-hour or 24-hour format) or to show a mathematical ratio, do *not* put any spaces around the colon.

8:15 PM (20:15)

The bomb exploded at 09:23:09.

The ratio of boys to girls in our math class is 3:1.

[9.2.2] Colon follows a complete sentence

When using the colon in sentences to introduce something, it should always follow a complete sentence (exceptions in [9.6] and [9.7]). Do not use a colon if one or more items in a list it is introducing are required to complete the sentence.

[CORRECT]

My wife gave me a list of spices to buy: oregano, thyme, sage, turmeric, cayenne pepper.

Multiple emotions coursed through me in rapid sequence: sadness over my brother's death, anger at the junkie who had sold him the drugs, guilt that I hadn't seen the signs of his addiction.

She turned around: full dark hair, wonderfully prominent cheekbones on a tanned face, captivating brown eyes.

[INCORRECT]

My wife gave me a list of spices to buy that included: oregano, thyme, sage, turmeric, cayenne pepper. (The list completes the sentence, so do not use a colon in that case.)

She turned around and I saw: full dark hair, wonderfully prominent cheekbones on a tanned face, captivating brown eyes. (same reason as above)

[9.2.3] Capitalizing after a colon

The CMOS says to capitalize after a colon only when it introduces a direct quotation or if what follows is a complete sentence, but not all authorities agree on this. The writer has flexibility. We recommend not capitalizing short sentences or phrases after the colon, but longer, complete sentences look better if capitalized.

[CORRECT]

I now faced a bigger problem: what do I do next? (short sentence)

Everyone knows the famous first line from Hamlet's soliloquy: "To be or not to be." (capitalize because it's a quotation)

Here's how I see it happening: we lie and deny being there. (short sentence)

Here's how he saw it happening: He could lie and tell them he found the mysterious, black stone outside the cave, or he could tell the truth and find himself explaining things he didn't want to explain. (long sentence)

He showed up at the wedding underdressed: The light blue, Oxford button-down shirt and navy tie were fine, but the jeans and sneakers didn't cut it. (long sentence)

In college you carry a notebook to class for two reasons: so the professors won't think you're cocky, and to record significant phone numbers. (no cap on "so" because an incomplete sentence follows)

[9.3] Colon to introduce

[9.3.1] Colon introduces a list or explanation

The most common use of the colon is to introduce a list, description, definition, or explanation. Do not use a colon if a list is introduced by a phrase like "such as."

Don't confuse the colon with the semicolon. The semicolon joins two related or parallel ideas; the colon indicates an expansion or explanation of one idea.

[CORRECT]

I made the mistake of inviting John for dinner, forgetting that he advocates a see-food diet: he sees food and eats it. (explanation follows colon)

Fred's explanation of the accident was as follows: the truck ran the red light and tried to stop, but it still smacked into the left rear of his car. (an explanation follows the colon)

Adrian Shadowhawk liked two things more than being alive: being a whiz at the latest computer technology, and being a vampire who knew how to use his hacking skills to the best advantage. (details follow the colon)

When one reviewer of his novel said that the ending was too *deus ex machina*, he figured he'd better look up the term: an unexpected, improbable, or artificial device or event introduced in a work of fiction to resolve a dilemma. Basically, it meant he'd pulled a rabbit out of his hat for the ending. (a definition follows the colon)

Multiple emotions coursed through me in rapid sequence: sadness over my brother's death, anger at the junkie who had sold him the drugs, guilt that I hadn't seen the signs of his addiction. (a list, emotions in this case, follows the colon)

[INCORRECT]

For dinner, my wife cooked: steak, mashed potatoes, steamed asparagus, buttered carrots, homemade rolls. (a complete sentence must precede the colon).

I like thick soups such as: cream of mushroom and New England clam chowder. (such as)

[9.3.2] Colon to precede a logical consequence

The colon can also precede a logical consequence. In this use, as well as preceding a list, it often replaces introductory words like "namely," "for example," and "that is."

Alice finally understood why her solution was not working: she'd used the wrong approach to the problem. (optionally capitalize "she")

[9.3.3] Appositive following a colon

In some cases, what follows a colon may be an appositive.

The envelope had no sender's name, only the printed initial, "Z" with a dash through it, and country of origin: England. ("England" is the appositive for "country of origin.")

[9.4] Colon to separate

The separating colon will not appear often in fiction, and this use does not count as overuse.

a mathematical ratio (4:3)

hours, minutes, and seconds in expressing time (13:24:05).

business letter salutations (Dear Sir:)

to separate a title from a subtitle (*Star Wars Episode IV: A New Hope*)

to denote chapter and verse of the Bible (Genesis 1:2)

in some plays to reference the act and scene (*Hamlet*, IV:ii)

* * *

ADVANCED: COLON

[9.5] Colon to pull the reader forward

In fiction, the colon can be used to pull the reader forward or to emphasize what follows. As we saw in [9.3], it introduces an elaboration or explanation. It can also introduce a revelation, or it may indicate that the answer to a question follows. Some of the examples below bend the rules. We've marked them.

> She wasn't sure which surprised her more: the remark itself, or her normally stuffy history professor pulling a presumed joke out of thin air.

> From one of the rundown houses raised voices pierced the night air: shouting, cursing, blaming.

> Ben scooted himself up in the chair and checked his watch: 11:53 P.M.

> They convinced others that fear among the humans would increase and that vampires would eventually be hunted on a large scale. Their solution: kill off humans before they killed us off. (bends the rules because a fragment precedes the colon)

> Wait, he might have a way out of this. This guard didn't know him, so: "Okay, my father doesn't know I'm here yet. Here's the story. I stayed with a 'friend' over the weekend and wasn't home." (bends the rules because "so" leaves the sentence open)

> The camera zoomed in closer. The door opened and someone he knew well ran out of the house: the Shadowhawk kid, the one he'd tortured for Hayes late last year.

> Scary thing: When Adam vanished, he took with him a database listing the location of vampires throughout the world. Scarier thing: Adam was a human without a conscience. (bends the rules because a fragment precedes the colon)

> Jake read from his notebook, "Name: Jefferson Scott Madison. Place of residence: Fort Bragg, North Carolina. Age: Twenty-two. Height: Six-four. Weight: One-ninety. Major: Biology, marine concentration. Minors: Art and Literature. Marital status: ...Single."

Monday, first day of class: The professor (Jake) greeted us, took attendance, picked up his chalk, and began. (bends the rules)

He closed his eyes and imagined the epitaph on his tombstone: Here lies f-ing stupid Adrian Shadowhawk.

He saw only one way for this assault to end: in a man-made rain of fire.

Because the colon emphasizes what follows it and pulls the reader forward, use it only when that's your intent. Otherwise, use a different punctuation mark. The following are all acceptable.

Stavan held out the sack of coins to the assassin: he hoped it was enough.

Stavan held out the sack of coins to the assassin; he hoped it was enough.

Stavan held out the sack of coins to the assassin. He hoped it was enough.

Stavan held out the sack of coins to the assassin—he hoped it was enough.

We've occasionally seen the colon used as a strong transition. Again, it bends the rules to do so, but it serves this purpose well in fiction.

After listening to all the arguments against a direct assault, he sat in silence for several seconds. Then: "Who is willing to act as bait?"

He'd kill the underlings first. Then: their leader.

[9.6] Colon to format dialogue

Consider this way to format an online chat in fiction.

Hack_attack_911: *hackers rule! what u need fangman*

Fangman: *looking for a ghost*

Hack_attack_911: *what u got*

You can use this technique with good effect in a short passage to show back-and-forth dialogue. Quotation marks are unnecessary here. (See chapter 15.)

She said: You said you went out with Nick.
He said: Nicki.
She said: And you slept with her.
He said: I slept.
She said: In the same bed.
He said: But not *with* her. I was too drunk.

[9.7] Colon following a list

Some authorities would say that a dash is preferable to the colon when a list comes first, but a colon is justifiable, if a bit more formal.

Extra shirt, clean socks, clean underwear, deodorant: I stuffed those into my backpack and was set for my two-day adventure.

Extra shirt, clean socks, clean underwear, deodorant—I stuffed those into my backpack and was set for my two-day adventure.

=====

Adrian put his hands on his hips and glared at Eli. "One, don't feed on humans without their permission; two, don't kill humans; three, don't change them: I didn't break any of your be-nice-to-humans commandments."

"What about the fourth one? Don't let them know you're a vampire."

"Yeah, well, when you're taking advantage of the snack permission they just gave you, it's kinda hard to hide that."

=====

NOTE: In this last example, we used semicolons in place of commas to separate the list items because they contain other commas.

[9.8] Colon vs. em-dash

Do not confuse a colon with the dash (em-dash). A dash is used to interrupt or to *separate* a phrase from the rest of the sentence, not to link or introduce as the colon does. (See chapter 10.)

[INCORRECT] I'll buy you a beer and we can talk some more: if that's okay.

[CORRECT] I'll buy you a beer and we can talk some more—if that's okay.

Here's a great example from Dickens' *Great Expectations* that also illustrates [9.7].

> He was gobbling mincemeat, meatbone, bread, cheese, and pork pie, all at once: staring distrustfully while he did so at the mist all round us, and often stopping—even stopping his jaws—to listen.

[9.9] Colon or comma?

Where you have the choice of a colon or a comma, which should you use? The best advice we have heard is that colons are noisier and more distracting. Therefore, use them only when necessary.

CHAPTER TEN

DASH

[10.1] Many types of dashes

The punctuation term "dash" includes at least *six* different pieces of punctuation (all different from the hyphen) that all have different uses: figure dash, minus sign, en-dash, em-dash, horizontal bar, swung dash (which looks like the tilde ~ but is different from it in use). Of these, only the en-dash and em-dash are of importance to most fiction writers. Interested readers can look the others up. Even though the hyphen and minus sign yield the same keyboard symbol, in the printing world they are different, but the difference is unimportant in fiction.

[10.2] Em-dash defined

The em-dash, sometimes called a long dash, gets its name from the printing world where typesetters originally made it the width of the letter "m." Not all fonts today follow this rule. In Times New Roman the em-dash is about 1.5 times as long as the letter em. Hereafter, we'll use *dash* to refer to the em-dash unless stated otherwise.

[10.3] En-dash defined

Comparable to the em-dash, the en-dash was originally set to be the width of the letter *n*. You learned in chapter 8 [8.6] that one use of the en-dash is to show number ranges. It has several other uses that we won't concern ourselves with here. The hyphen will suffice for fiction writers.

[10.4] How to enter an em-dash or en-dash

On typewriters, the only way to show an em-dash was with a double hyphen (--). Even on computers, some writers still prefer to use this approach for manuscripts in progress. This is your choice in, but in your final, published work should replace those with true em-dashes to avoid formatting problems in e-books.

To enter these dashes directly from the keyboard use ALT 0150 (en-dash) and ALT 0151 (em-dash). (See [INTRO.3.1] regarding ALT codes.)

On Mac computers, for the en-dash, hold down the OPTION key and press the minus key. For the em-dash hold down the OPTION and SHIFT keys and press the minus key.

NOTE: Do *not* put spaces on either side of an em-dash or en-dash.

Refer to [INTRO.3.3] for setting MS Word to replace a double hyphen (--) with an em-dash automatically. You can also manually convert these to em-dashes with the search & replace function. The automatic and manual replace work properly most of the time, but they're not perfect. Always check the final manuscript to be sure. Using em-dashes from the start will ensure that you do not have to fix and check them later.

[10.5] Em-dash in UK English

In UK English, an en-dash with a single space on each side of it may be used instead of an em-dash. We do see many UK English writers using the hyphen instead of an en-dash. That's an acceptable alternative, but the en-dash is preferable, and it's the *only* place where it's permissible to put spaces around a hyphen.

[AMERICAN] Driving home that night in the snowstorm—in a complete whiteout—was very scary. (em-dashes, no spaces)

[UK] Driving home that night in the snowstorm – in a complete whiteout – was very scary. (en-dash with spaces around it)

[10.6] Uses of the em-dash—options of expression

Some writers confuse the roles of the em-dash and ellipsis (see chapter 11), as if they're simply two options for the same thing. They are not even close to being the same.

The dash is used to set off elements of a sentence and is stronger than a comma in this regard. It has two basic uses: separation and interruption.

As a separator, the em-dash sets off a word, phrase, or clause from the rest of the sentence, either as a parenthetical or for emphasis.

As an interrupter, the em-dash provides a strong break in the sentence, such as a break in a character's thoughts or speech (see [10.6.3] and chapter 15). These breaks may occur anywhere in the sentence.

NOTE: The dash *separates*. It does not join. Do not use it to join independent clauses.

[CORRECT]

My boss, the esteemed Dr. Ferraro, has been pissed lately at his grad students who—through no fault of theirs—have not produced anything he can publish.

My boss (the esteemed Dr. Ferraro) has been pissed lately at his grad students who—through no fault of theirs—have not produced anything he can publish.

My boss—the esteemed Dr. Ferraro—has been pissed lately at his grad students who, through no fault of theirs, have not produced anything he can publish.

I came to attention—force of habit—and stared at the body behind the unfamiliar voice.

He hadn't brought up the job again during the trip—just as well, because I knew I didn't want it.

I'm not saying we should forget it—I'm not—just that we pick up the discussion tomorrow when we're all less tired and can think more clearly.

Evan ran his fingers over the surface of the object—they dragged slightly against its matte finish—and handed it back.

[INCORRECT]

Evan ran his fingers over the surface of the object—they dragged slightly against its matte finish. (This improperly joins two independent clauses, unlike the previous example where the clause is a parenthetical.)

[CORRECT]

Jake ran his fingers over the surface. They dragged slightly against its matte finish.

Dashes highlight the element more strongly and give it more visibility than putting commas or parentheses around it would. They may also help to unclutter a comma-cluttered sentence. In some cases, the element set off with dashes may be a parenthetical. The choice between em-dashes and parentheses is one of desired style and ultimate effect in a given piece.

[CORRECT]

A tall, distinguished, haggard gentleman—a professorial stereotype—with an Oxford British accent proudly stepped forward.

Dr. Allen glanced into the newly remodeled waiting room where at least a dozen people sat—half of them kids and two crying.

As far as he knew, he hadn't committed any major infractions of Eli's Rules—no more than usual, anyway.

Jason had been dressed and ready an hour ago: only slightly sagged jeans—he wasn't into showing off his butt—and an oversized, white T-shirt.

He believed—no, he was certain—that he was right, no matter what they said.

Some of these sentences could be recast without the dashes for a different emphasis. The dash gives the writer options for expression.

[10.6.1] Dash to replace a colon

The dash can often be used in place of a colon. In this role it offers a stronger emphasis than a comma and less separation and a less formal tone than a colon.

[CORRECT]

He only ever asked for one thing: respect. (more formal)

He only ever asked for one thing—respect.

After his flight had to be rescheduled, Jeff had a real problem: could he still get to the meeting in time?

After his flight had to be rescheduled, Jeff had a real problem—could he still get to the meeting in time?

[10.6.2] Dashes with parentheticals

Dashes may be used in place of commas for parentheticals when you want to emphasize the parenthetical. They may be used instead of parentheses (if you've chosen not to use actual parentheses), but they are stronger separators than either commas or parentheses.

Pain lanced up my arm, like stubbing your toe and smacking your shin at the same instant—multiplied a thousand times.

Pain lanced up my arm, like stubbing your toe and smacking your shin at the same instant (multiplied a thousand times).

Pain lanced up my arm, like stubbing your toe and smacking your shin at the same instant, multiplied a thousand times.

He picked up a hypodermic device, with a needle, not the transdermal spray I expected from advanced alien technology.

He picked up a hypodermic device—with a needle, not the transdermal spray I expected from advanced alien technology.

[10.6.3] Dash to interrupt dialogue or thoughts

In dialogue, the dash is used to signal a break, interruption, or omission, such as when the speaker interrupts himself or is interrupted. This also applies to a character's thoughts. We'll expand on this in chapters 12 and 15. Here are some examples to illustrate this use.

=====

"Let me handle the details," Adam said. "Tell me where to direct the money. I'll see it arrives safely and secretly at its destination. There is one stipulation, Reverend. This will create a partnership between us. In return for my seven-figure contributions—"
The Reverend coughed.
"—I'll expect your full cooperation on certain matters."

=====

Eric took the first leap into the unknown and could have been seriously injured. He should have stopped after that. "It was my idea—"
"But I convinced him to go through with it," Jack said.

=====

"What's—" Emily said.

Sarah slapped a hand over her sister's mouth and with a rapid headshake pushed her behind the bookshelves.

=====

Bergmann didn't grasp the meaning immediately. "Sir? You expect us to test the product on ourselves?"

"You have the antidote."

"You never told us to develop—"

"In that case, I suggest you exercise your collective brains over the next few days to develop one as if the duration of your life expectancy depended on it."

=====

Shaking, heart racing, Maureen sat in her car, the engine still running, and looked over at the other car, overturned in the ditch. *One second. I only glanced at the radio for one—*

She pulled out her cell phone to call 911.

[10.7] Overuse of the dash

Some writers are very fond of dashes and use them to excess. As with any mark other than periods and commas, too many can distract the reader and lessen their impact. Stick with the old standbys of commas and periods for the bulk of your punctuation and use the dash only when it's the best choice. One exception to multiple dashes on a page is where characters keep interrupting one another—or various things interrupt the dialogue—possibly in a high-action or tense scene. But be careful of overusing this technique.

[MESSY] My boss—the esteemed Dr. Ferraro—has been pissed lately at his grad students who—through no fault of theirs—have not produced anything he can publish.

We recently saw the dash used to excess deliberately as a matter of style in a story that almost read as a stream-of-consciousness piece. The piece was strong and well done and the dashes (used in place of most commas) gave the piece a flavor that commas would not. It took some getting used to, and we suspect that more than a few readers would be put off by it. Again, use care with such style choices.

CHAPTER ELEVEN

ELLIPSIS

[11.1] Ellipsis definition

The ellipsis (or ellipsis points) is a series of three (and only three!) periods used to indicate missing or omitted text in a quotation or pauses or trailing off in thoughts or dialogue.

[11.2] Ellipsis formatting

Current convention (and the CMOS) says to use three periods with a single space between each and a space before and after the three dots. All three of the periods must appear together on the same line. An ellipsis may occur at the end of a line but should not occur at the start of a line.

[CORRECT]
If the knowledge became known it would...
damage my reputation.

[INCORRECT]
If the knowledge became known it would
... damage my reputation.

=====

The ellipsis with spaces between them works fine in printed text where the printer controls the page layout. Word processors and e-reader software have a problem with this convention because they use spaces to determine where to break a line. Unlike in print books, the text in e-books is not fixed in location on the page (called "reflowable text"). The font type and size can also be changed by the user. Therefore, a particular ellipsis may fall anywhere on a line, regardless of its placement in the original manuscript. When it falls at the end of a line, the software will break it at an appropriate space, causing the ellipsis points to split between the end of one line and the start of the next.

[UGLY] If the knowledge became known it would..
. damage my reputation.

=====

Word processors have special characters called nonbreaking spaces to prevent this behavior, but not all e-book software may recognize these special spaces. For this reason, we recommend—contrary to what the CMOS says—that you use either three *unspaced* periods ... or that you insert the single ellipsis symbol, which is treated properly by e-book software.

> In MS Word on a PC enter the ellipsis symbol with ALT 0133. (See [INTRO.3.1] regarding ALT codes.) Alternatively, hold both the CTL and ALT keys and press the period.

> On a Mac, hold the OPTION key and press the semicolon key.

We also recommend that you *not* put a space before the ellipsis because it could be split off to the beginning next line (which looks awkward). We *do* recommended a space *after* the ellipsis because this ensures that the ellipsis does not join the two words it comes between, thus treating them as one word.

Advanced formatting techniques for the e-book may be able to avoid these and other issues, but unless you have that capability, our approach will help ensure cleanly formatted e-books.

[11.3] Ellipsis to show omitted text

Traditionally the ellipsis is used to show the omission of words in a piece of quoted text, such as you might do in a paper you're writing. We show examples here, but this use of the ellipsis is rare in fiction.

> [ORIGINAL] The important thing is not to stop questioning. Curiosity has its own reason for existing. One cannot help but be in awe when he contemplates the mysteries of eternity, of life, of the marvelous structure of reality. It is enough if one tries merely to comprehend a little of this mystery every day. Never lose a holy curiosity. (Albert Einstein)

> [SHORTENED] The important thing is not to stop questioning.... Never lose a holy curiosity.

NOTE: The "extra" period in the ellipsis above includes the period at the end of the sentence as the *first* of the four dots.

> [ORIGINAL] When in the Course of human events, it becomes necessary for one people to dissolve the political bands which have connected them with another, and to assume among the

powers of the earth, the separate and equal station to which the Laws of Nature and of Nature's God entitle them, a decent respect to the opinions of mankind requires that they should declare the causes which impel them to the separation.

[SHORTENED] When in the Course of human events, it becomes necessary for one people to dissolve the political bands which have connected them with another... they should declare the causes which impel them to the separation.

NOTE: When showing the omission of a long passage or paragraph, put an ellipsis in square brackets [...] on a separate line. The CMOS uses this method, but some other style guides omit the brackets. Again, this is use is rare in fiction. We omit an example of this here. The CMOS provides examples if you require this technique.

[11.4] Ellipsis to show a hesitation

Since ellipsis points are used to show an omission, in fiction this is extended to show a hesitation or trailing off in speech, an unfinished thought, a pause to think of the right word, or a pause for dramatic effect.

Do not confuse this with interruptions in speech that would use a dash. The ellipsis in dialogue represents a hesitation or tailing off on the speaker's part, not an interruption by someone or something else. We deal further with the ellipsis in dialogue in chapter 15.

[EM-DASH= interruption by another speaker or event]

[ELLIPSIS= interruption or hesitation by the one speaking]

Her breathing had become less labored, but the tears were starting. She looked at her handcuffed attacker, then at the stranger who had saved her, then at the police officers. "If h-he hadn't been here..."

He couldn't remember when he'd last spoken with her. Yes, she would listen. Whether she could help... "I'll call her," he said.

For a moment, Ben appreciated Seth's rambling because it took his mind off why he'd come here. "Seth..." He swallowed. "I want..." He exhaled, feeling the emotion rising again. "I *need* your help."

He wasn't sure what to make of the order. "Terminate with extreme prejudice" seemed so... barbaric.

In the past month he'd gone from a stay-out-all-night, do-as-he-pleased, party animal to... a responsible, stay-at-home, big brother. No wonder his friends had stopped calling him.

When they arrived, all the volunteers were healthy. Yesterday, five were sick enough to be bedridden. This morning... two of them died.

Here are two famous lines from the 1931 classic movie *Dracula* that illustrate an ellipsis for dramatic effect.

"I am... Dracula. I bid you... welcome."

"I never drink... wine."

* * *

ADVANCED: ELLIPSIS

[11.5] Other punctuation with ellipses

Sometimes ellipsis points are used indicate an incomplete sentence, but when the ellipsis does end a sentence, we have to know where to put the terminal punctuation of the sentence. You'll find conflicting answers. The CMOS says to put the punctuation *before* the ellipsis dots. In the examples below, the first of four dots is the period.

"Uh, I guess so.... We can meet here after it gets dark...." Tom thought about it for a moment. "Be sure no one follows you."

"How?..." Realization shone in Seth's expression. "You want me to... change him? Into a vampire? You can't be serious."

David abruptly turned and marched to the door. "David,... if this is your answer, we're done," his father said.

In the last example, we put a comma before the ellipsis because "David" is a vocative (direct address) and a comma is normally required after it. Our research did not turn up a definitive answer for this, though, mostly due to the lack of examples. You could omit the comma because the context makes the direct address clear, but we recommend inserting it for consistency.

"Jeff, I understand that Connor and Sebastian are okay with it," Carl said. "But Drake... what about him?" (Here, Drake is someone being spoken about, not being addressed, but it might be better to reword as "But... what about Drake?" so the meaning is clear.)

"Jeff, I understand that Connor and Sebastian are okay with it," Carl said. He looked at Drake. "But, Drake,... how do you feel?" (Here, Drake is being addressed.)

"There's something you ought to know about your great-grandfather. How can I put this?... He was an evil man."

"Very nice to meet you, Mr., ah, Mrs.... Uh, nice to make your acquaintance." (The period used with *Mrs.* is part of the abbreviation, not the end of the sentence because the sentence trails off and doesn't end.)

[11.6] Ellipsis to indicate unheard parts of dialogue

In fiction, as in real life, a character may overhear pieces of a conversation. He might be too far away, in a noisy environment, or hearing one side of a telephone conversation.

=====

Julia stood next to the open kitchen door, listening to her brother talking on the phone.
"I can't right now.... My father is still here, that's why.... I don't know when. What?... Yes, I'll call you as soon he leaves."

=====

[11.7] Ellipsis to show the passage of time

Example:

The cruelty of Suspension for prisoners like Rephet meant that, although their bodies had no biologic needs, their minds were kept active and fully conscious to watch in torment the inexorable passage of Hathan's three seasons that they could no longer partake of. Cascading down the blue snowfalls in Cold Season... Embracing the green upwellings in the Growing Season... In-flight matings on the backs of Raspora in the Harvest Season...

[11.8] Ellipsis vs. dash

Compare the use of an ellipsis to express an unfinished sentence with a dash to show an interrupted one in the two examples below.

NOTE: When the dash ends a sentence or fragment, put a space between it and the next sentence.

> They were coming; they'd be here any minute. Paul stared at the gun on the table. He couldn't do what they asked. He needed time to think, to find another...

> They were coming; they'd be here any minute. Paul stared at the gun on the table. He couldn't do what they asked. He needed time to think, to— The door burst open.

When leaving sentences unfinished, as in the first example, make sure readers understand the implication and don't simply wonder what the character was going to do or think. We assume Paul means "to find another *option*." In the second case, we are less concerned with what was left unsaid because the interruption takes precedence. The reader can fill in that blank.

Study the following dialogue passage, which shows ellipses used for both trailing and halting speech.

=====

> "Where's J?" Drake asked Ben.
> "In the bedroom... Crying, I think."
> "What's wrong?" Adrian asked.
> Ben shut his eyes. "Maybe you can talk to him. He won't listen to me."
> Adrian headed to Jonathan's room. "Little bro?" Jonathan had his face buried in the pillow.
> "M-my mom... h-hates me."
> Adrian sat on the bed and put his hand on Jonathan's back. "No, she doesn't."
> "Sh-she th-thinks... I'm... a... m-m-monster."

=====

Jonathan's broken speech is shown in two ways. His halting speech is done with ellipses to show pauses and hesitations (not interruptions), while his stuttered words are done with hyphens because he's not pausing deliberately there.

146

In the following, ellipses are used for dropped, overheard dialogue, and a dash shows the interruption of that dialogue. The italics indicate the sound and direct thoughts. (See [14.3.6])

=====

Isaac had hoped to learn who was behind the theft and when they expected the buyer to show up, but the men were too far away and the noises in the warehouse made it difficult to hear.

"... said... he'd be here at... s—" *Beep-beep-beep* "thirty with our money."

Damn pallet trucks! He hadn't heard the hour. It was 6:20 now. If their contact was coming in ten minutes, his own men wouldn't be here in time. If it was 7:30...

The following passages show the differences between the ellipsis and the dash.

"Just poker. Unmarked deck, straight dealing. Honest—"

"You didn't use your telepathic ability even once?"

"You know mine's poor. Besides, I promise I didn't use it... once. Do you think we ever could, like, communicate completely without talking? That'd be so cool. Maybe we could find a way to make mine stronger."

=====

"Becoming a vampire isn't a cure-all. He might recover completely, or partially, or not at all. Or... it could make him worse."

Ben's shoulders slumped. "God, Seth, why did you have to say that?"

"I want you to understand all the risks. The change is physically and emotionally stressful. I've heard of a couple of vampire doctors in Europe. I could contact—"

"No!" Ben found himself panting. "This has to happen now... before I change my mind."

=====

You may be thinking that the ellipsis is like a "super comma" in terms of its pause value. This is true in a way, but we hope it's not necessary to remind you *not* to overuse the ellipsis. We've seen writers do it, and it makes for a poor presentation of one's writing.

CHAPTER TWELVE

QUOTATION MARKS

[12.1] Quotation mark basics

Despite being widely used as punctuation, we've left quotation marks until almost last because their usage for multiple purposes makes them one of the more complex marks to understand.

[12.1.1] Terminology

The initial quotation mark is termed an *open quote* and the one at the end is a *close quote* (not "closed quote"). On a typewriter or computer keyboard, the open and close quote are the same mark, sometimes called *straight quotes* to distinguish them from the *smart quotes* (" ") that we'll discuss in [12.10]. Note the direction the smart quotes face.

SIDE NOTE: You can force smart/curly quotes if you have Word set to straight quotes, but you cannot force straight quotes if you have the "smart quotes replacement" turned on. Why would you want to force straight quotes? When you need to put quotes in a web link (as in a blog), you must use straight quotes or the link won't work.

Further, Word does not distinguish between the single quote and an apostrophe. When using an apostrophe to start a word (e.g., *'cause* as a contraction for *because*, you must enter the close quote manually because Word will enter it in the wrong direction ('cause). Therefore, you cannot just use smart quotes all the time even though they're the accepted convention. There will be times when you have to modify them manually.

[12.1.2] US/UK conventions

In US English usage, it is standard to use the double quotation mark ("). UK English usually (but not always) uses the single quote mark ('), the same as the apostrophe, which they also call an inverted comma. The placement of other punctuation relative to the quotation marks varies between the US and UK. Even more confusing is that practices in UK English are not always consistent. Some use the double quote instead of the single quote.

[12.1.3] Other punctuation with quote marks

In US English most punctuation marks go *inside* the quote marks: comma, period, question mark, exclamation mark, ellipsis, dash. The semicolon and colon go *outside* the quote marks. (See [12.6])

[12.2] Uses of quotation marks

Quotation marks have five basic uses, all of which may occur in fiction.

[12.2.1] Quotation marks for direct speech

Quotation marks are most commonly used to indicate direct speech (spoken words in dialogue, not thoughts). We cover thoughts in chapter 14.

Because the punctuation of dialogue is a complex topic, we have written a separate chapter (15) to deal with it. For now, we'll cover only the essentials.

Begin a passage of direct speech with an open quote (" or "). The dialogue follows that and ends with a close quote (" or ").

Dialogue may have a dialogue tag associated with it to tell who the speaker is. Tags go outside the quotation marks and are normally separated from the dialogue (never a period), but a question mark or exclamation mark may replace the comma. A dialogue tag is part of the sentence. If a tag follows the dialogue, put the period *after* the tag, not before it.

"Owen isn't going to the party at Dave's house tonight."

"I'll meet you there," Mike said.

"Can I bring my friend Pavel?" Claire asked.

"What a cool car!" Jason said. He loved Corvettes, especially silver ones.

Steve said, "I have to study tonight. If I don't get at least a C on the math final, I'll fail the course for sure."

"I thought they'd never leave," Jen said. "Let me handle this."

[12.2.2] Quotation marks for direct quotes

In any type of writing, material quoted from another source is always enclosed in quotation marks, including whatever punctuation appeared in the original.

> He told me that the famous Sherlock Holmes quote "How often have I said to you that when you have eliminated the impossible, whatever remains, *however improbable*, must be the truth?" comes from the story "The Sign of Four."

[12.2.3] Quotation marks with certain titles & names

In chapter 14 we'll discuss the use of italics vs. quotation marks for the titles of various kinds of works, but in general, use italics for longer works: books, movies, TV shows, magazines, record albums, and plays. Art objects and works of art are generally considered longer works as well.

For shorter works (poems, short stories, song titles), use quotation marks. Also use quotation marks for titles of sections, chapters, or individual pieces within longer works.

Well-known and famous works, such as The Gettysburg Address, The Declaration of Independence, and the Bible require nothing to set them off.

Use quotes for nicknames and false titles: Nat "King" Cole, Charlie "Lucky" Luciano, Bruce "The Boss" Springsteen.

[12.2.4] Quotation marks to give special attention

When you want to set off a word or phrase or to make it stand out from the rest of words around it, you may put it in quotes or in italic type. Italic type is the preferred method, but use the one that seems best for the situation.

> *Freedom of Speech* doesn't always mean we can say whatever we want without consequences. (option with italics)

> "Freedom of Speech" doesn't always mean we can say whatever we want without consequences. (option with quotes)

> The word "phthisis" refers to any wasting disease of the body but usually of the lungs. It can also refer to an asthmatic

condition. The "ph" is silent, which makes the word pronounced almost like "this is." (We could use also italics here instead of quotes.)

The next two examples each use both methods to differentiate certain elements.

In the sentence *My younger brother, Frank, gave me a present*, "Frank" is an appositive that further defines "my younger brother" in a nonrestrictive way, meaning I have only one younger brother and his name is Frank.

Some German words look identical to their English equivalent and mean the same but are pronounced differently. *Butter* means "butter" and *Hand* means "hand" in both languages. *Schuh* is the German word for "shoe" and is pronounced almost the same as the English word. But the German word *Bad* means "bath."

[12.2.5] Quotation marks for different level of usage

When used to show a different level of usage or meaning, such quotation marks are known as *scare quotes*. They're also called *air quotes* or *finger quotes* when used in person by a speaker indicating such quote marks with the fingers. In this usage they may convey the meaning of *so-called* or *alleged*, sometimes with a note of sarcasm attached.

At the meeting, some of the city's trash collectors were talking "trash."

Normal people are not always "normal" in some people's eyes.

He pointed the gun at me in an attempt to "persuade" me to change my mind.

A "new" car doesn't always mean it's never been driven before.

When he said he bought a "new" car, he meant it was new to him, not a brand-new car.

The princess declared that she would never marry a commoner because they were so "common."

The careful writer uses scare quotes only when necessary, not every time the writer thinks they're needed. Overused scare quotes become intrusive and may mark the writer as an amateur.

[12.3] Single quotes vs. double quotes

We've seen some writers assume that single quote marks have a different level of significance from double quotes. For example, they incorrectly use single quotes for scare quotes. Single and double quotes have the *same* level of meaning.

> [INCORRECT] He pointed the gun at me in an attempt to 'persuade' me to change my mind. (use double quotes)

See [12.4] for the appropriate—and only—use of single quotation marks in US English.

* * *

ADVANCED: QUOTATION MARKS

[12.4] Quotes within quotes

[12.4.1] How to nest quotes

Because quoted material can be nested inside other quoted material, a combination of double and single quote marks is used to avoid reader confusion. In US English, always use double quotes for the first layer. If it is necessary to use a second layer of quotation marks (dialogue or quoted material within dialogue or quoted material), put that new material in single quote marks.

If you need a third layer, use double quotes again, and so forth. It's rare to need more than two layers of quotes in fiction, but if you do, simply keep alternating between double and single.

NOTE: In UK English, when single quotes are used for the first layer, double quotes are used for the next layer (quotes within quotes), the reverse of US English.

> "Even though I'm not in the military, my boss is. He keeps trying to enlist me, and I keep telling him, 'Captain's bars would be nice.'"

"Donna asked me if I had read the Robert Frost poem 'Mending Wall' assigned for English class."

"What, no 'Take me to your leader'?" Mark asked. (Note the question mark placement. It belongs to the outer quote, not the inner one. See [12.4.2])

I told them, "Arion said he would continue to search for Trax's father, but couldn't promise anything. Trax claimed he knew everything his father knew. Arion told him, 'In that you are wrong.' Trax said nothing more after that."

Here is an example of three levels of quote marks:

"I asked Jason last night how his term paper on *Romeo and Juliet* was coming and he said, 'Did you know it's got some really smutty lines? One passage reads "Stuffed, as they say, with honorable parts, proportioned as one's heart could wish a man." It doesn't take much imagination to figure out what *that* means. Maybe if we tell the School Board, they'll put all of Shakespeare on their "banned books" list.' I told him, 'We can only hope.'"

This example is more convoluted than most writers would write, but it illustrates how to nest quoted material.

[12.4.2] Punctuating nested quotes

When deciding where to place the punctuation with tags where nested quotes are used, it's necessary to look at which part the punctuation belongs to. If a verb follows the quotes, do not use a comma. Look at these examples.

"Arion told him, 'In that you are wrong.'" (comma after "him" because "Arion told him" is a speech tag telling us who spoke.)

One passage reads "Stuffed, as they say, with honorable parts." ("One passage reads" is not a speech tag, so no comma after it.)

"You'll be sorry if you don't accept the offer" was Sarah's advice to me. (no comma because a verb follows)

"Use the right word, not its second cousin" is a superb piece of writing advice, courtesy of Mark Twain. (verb follows)

"No matter what I say, they'll have an attitude of 'What arrogance!'" (not a tag, no comma)

EXCEPTION: When a long, *complete* sentence introduces or follows quoted material, a colon may be appropriate. Otherwise, use a comma.

President Franklin Roosevelt inspired many Americans with this statement: "The only thing we have to fear is fear itself."

President Franklin Roosevelt inspired many Americans when he said, "The only thing we have to fear is fear itself." (introductory sentence is not complete)

"I think it would be a good idea.": Mahatma Gandhi said that when asked what he thought of Western civilization.

NOTE: When talking about characters reading signs, notes, or letters, be sure you use "read" not "said." Signs and notes don't talk, but use common sense with the wording.

When John left a note on the table that told me "Keep off the grass," I wasn't sure if it was a reminder that our neighbor's new dog liked to do its business in our yard or a warning not to smoke any of his marijuana.

[12.5] Straight & smart (curly) quotation marks

The choice of straight or curly quotes is up to you, but in published material, curly quotes generally look better. Be careful, though, when preparing your manuscript in a word processing program and verify that all of open and close quotes are in the right direction.

[12.5.1] Automatic smart quote issues in MS Word

MS Word's default option is to use smart quotes. The problem is that it sometimes gets them wrong. For example, MS Word will do the following—

"I'm sorry but I can't go tonight. " (The final quote mark is backward because of the space after the period. MS Word expects the quote mark to follow the end punctuation directly. To fix, delete the wrong mark and the space and type the quote mark again, or insert it manually. (See [12.10.2])

"I'm sorry but—" (MS Word doesn't always recognize an em-dash or hyphen as a terminal mark and incorrectly uses an open quote. Fix it manually (see [12.5.2]) or, if you use the search and replace function in Word to convert straight quotes to smart quotes, Word gets them right (but always verify). See [INTRO.3.3] for how to disable smart quotes.

[12.5.2] Manual entry of smart quotes in MS Word

There are several manual ways to insert smart quotes or to fix ones that Word gets wrong. Using keyboard codes to enter them is the easiest fix on a PC (or Mac). (See [INTRO.3.1] on ALT codes.)

PC open single quote ('): ALT 0145 == Mac: OPTION]

PC close single quote ('): ALT 0146 == Mac: OPTION SHIFT]

PC open double quote ("): ALT 0147 == Mac: OPTION [

PC close double quote ("): ALT 0148 == Mac: OPTION SHIFT [

[12.6] Punctuation outside quotation marks

In dialogue, most of the time the additional punctuation goes inside the quote marks because it's part of the dialogue line. The convention is to keep the punctuation with the sentence it belongs to. Commas and periods always go inside the quotation marks, even with quotes within quotes.

Question marks and exclamation marks are placed depending on the situation. Our advice is to avoid confusing situations, but here are the rules when you have no other choice.

The placement of the ? or ! with regard to the quote marks depends on what the actual question or exclamation is.

[CORRECT]

John asked, "Can I go with you?" (Normal question)

"Did John say, 'I can go with you'?" (What John said is not a question, but the entire spoken line *is* a question.)

"Did John ask, 'Can I go with you?'" (When both are questions, don't double up on question marks.)

155

[INCORRECT] "Did John ask, 'Can I go with you?'?"

[CORRECT]

Do you agree with the saying, "Might makes right"? (Here you can leave out the period after *Might makes right* and just use the stronger question mark.)

Mark told me, "Can you believe Jason said 'I *am* going with you'?" (No comma after *said* because it's part of Mark's dialogue, not a dialogue tag.)

Don't be tempted to use an exclamation mark to indicate a more intense reaction from Jason. Instead, use an alternative:

Mark told me, "Jason actually *screamed*, 'I *am* going with you!' he said."

"Do you know the meaning of the Latin phrase 'veni, vidi, vici'?" Brian asked.

My brother claims that his high school sweetheart won his heart when she played Juliet opposite his Romeo and uttered that classic line "Romeo, Romeo! wherefore art thou Romeo?".

While the end punctuation in the last example may look weird, it is correct. The question mark belongs to the quoted material, which is then followed by a close quote.

However, the main sentence here is really *My brother claims ... uttered that classic line.* (Note how we used ellipsis points here to show the missing part of the sentence.) That sentence is a statement. Therefore, put the period for that sentence *after* the close quote.

NOTE: When the sentence *and* the quote are both questions, and the quote falls at the end as it does in the example, use only one question mark as shown below.

Is it true your brother claims that his high school sweetheart won his heart when she played Juliet opposite his Romeo and uttered that classic line "Romeo, Romeo! wherefore art thou Romeo?"

INTERESTING SIDE NOTE: Most people believe that famous line from *Romeo and Juliet* has Juliet asking Romeo where he is. Look closely at the punctuation of the line. At the beginning, Juliet is addressing Romeo. Note the comma of direct address. After the second "Romeo" an exclamation mark substitutes for a second comma. However, the expected comma of direct address before his name at the *end* of the sentence is missing. That's because it's not direct address. In this context, *wherefore* does not mean "where" but carries the more archaic meaning of "for what reason." Juliet isn't trying to find Romeo. She's asking *why* he's Romeo, one of the Montagues, a rival family of hers, the Capulets.

Colons and semicolons are placed outside the quotation marks unless they're a part of the dialogue, but we weren't able to come up with any reasonable dialogue examples ending with a colon or a semicolon to show this. Here are some examples using scare quotes.

Jackson claimed that he was an exception to the "rules"; they didn't apply to him.

I rolled my eyes when she told me about her "most epic life achievement": overcoming the immense burden of being the smartest person she knew.

Melissa said, "That's my 'most epic life achievement': overcoming the immense burden of being the smartest person I know." (This is an awkward example used solely to show the punctuation usage.)

[12.7] Miscellaneous advice regarding quotation marks

[12.7.1] Avoid complex punctuation situations

Even though we have tried to teach you how to deal with complex punctuation around quotation marks, we advise that if you find yourself in an uncertain situation, rework the passage to avoid the problem or an awkward sentence. If the reader encounters something bizarre, he may trip over it or stop to ponder it, and this is not a desirable outcome for your readers.

[12.7.2] Use quotes around long compound adjective phrases

Instead of hyphenating a long adjectival phrase, putting it in quotation marks makes it visually less distracting, but be sure it's worded so the reader understands it's adjectival phrase and not something in scare quotes.

My body began to tingle in that foreshadowing, calm-before-a-disaster way. (This would look odd in quotes)

Forty feet ahead was a ten-by-ten-foot-square opening. (Even though the phrase is long, this one would also look odd in quotes.)

This coming Sunday, I was graduating from college at my virginal best, having been scared spermless by the do-it-and-watch-it-rot Army training films thrust upon an impressionable, pubescent child of twelve. (Either way works here, but putting "*do it and watch it rot*" in quotes would also suggest a bit of irony.)

He shivered. Tonight was a little cool for his favorite "You've Mistaken Me For Someone Who Gives A Damn" T-shirt. (This would definitely look awkward if hyphenated. The quotes here also indicate that this describes what's written on the shirt, not the shirt itself.)

CHAPTER THIRTEEN

PARENTHESES, BRACKETS, BRACES

[13.1] Parentheses

In fiction, parentheses ( ) can be used to add supplemental, explanatory, or clarifying information or to add an aside by the narrator. They can also be used to provide the translation of foreign language words and dialogue for the reader.

> TIP: Foreign languages in fiction are fine if not overused. We feel it's better to avoid them unless their meaning can be deduced from the context. Otherwise, readers may find constant translations in parentheses annoying.

[13.1.1] Dashes vs. parentheses

Sometimes dashes are a better option for parenthetical expressions (or you can use commas). If you find parentheses preferable, you should establish their use early on and be consistent in employing them. As with dashes, don't overuse parentheses. When deciding between dashes and parentheses, be aware that dashes are more intrusive (see [10.6]), so keeping them to a minimum is advisable. In the last two examples below, one uses parentheses, one dashes. In the last one, parentheses would probably be a better option and yield less visual confusion than dashes. When choosing punctuation, always keep the visual appearance of the prose in mind. As we've said before, the purpose of punctuation is to make the writing and the author's intent clear to and easy on the reader.

> The Victorian-style, oak balustrade (Zoe called it a banister despite her sister's attempts to correct her.) was breathtaking.

> The Victorian-style, oak balustrade—Zoe called it a banister despite her sister's attempts to correct her—was breathtaking.

> The Victorian-style, oak balustrade, which Zoe called a banister despite her sister's attempts to correct her, was breathtaking.

> Our party consisted of two factions: those who knew what was going on (Kedda and Jake), and those who didn't (Jen-Varth, Trax, Enelle, and me).

Teddy followed the four vampire rules about dealing with humans: keep secret what you are (most of the time he did), don't change them into vampires (he'd never done that), don't kill them unless you have no other choice (he'd never killed anyone and didn't plan on doing so), and ask permission to feed on them. He usually obtained his blood from paid, volunteer-donor sources. Tonight was a justifiable exception.

Our brief, decision-making session had decided who would cross the Gate threshold: Trax, because the staff supposedly protected him—which it hadn't done before—and me, because we were entering a Magick world where my medallion should—according to Dayon—protect me.

[13.1.2] Nested parentheses

Parentheses can be nested for certain effects, satirical or comedic, for example. Some authorities warn against this nesting, and the CMOS recommends using square brackets [ ] inside parentheses instead of nesting a second set (see [13.3]). The CMOS suggestion might provide better visual impact for the reader as well as being less confusing than nesting parentheses. Avoid making the reader have to work to understand your intent.

In the following passage, nested parentheses add an interesting voice and an extra level of humor that dashes would not. Use this technique with discretion because it can quickly become annoying.

I first met Barclay Stevens by accident (more like a multi-car-pileup kind of accident) and our encounter was far from pleasant (he was an asshole (the asshole of assholes)), although I'd later come to realize that my first impression of him was wrong in the worst possible way (and what self-respecting vampire would be caught dead (or undead) with a name like "Barclay" anyway?).

Yep, Barclay Stevens was a vampire, but you couldn't tell by looking at him (true vampires don't have fangs or pasty complexions (he had a nice tan), and they aren't allergic to garlic (he loved a good garlic rub on his medium-rare steaks)). No, he was your least typical vampire (his sun-bleached blond hair made him look more like a surfer dude than a badass bloodsucker (all of which it made me question my preconceptions of a "typical" vampire)).

But you're probably wondering what unpleasantness accompanied our first encounter. It had nothing to do with Barclay being a vampire (unless you consider being a vampire a prerequisite to being an asshole).

=====

NOTE: Although this is a cool trick with the nested parentheses, this passage is a little difficult to read. You might have to read it a second time to appreciate it. We once saw an author use parentheses nested three deep in a single sentence of over 650 words! It added humor, but a high degree of writing skill is required to pull this off.

[13.2] Braces

Braces are rarely used in fiction. Unless you need to include mathematical expressions or computer program lines in your writing (which you might), you likely won't need braces.

If the writer needs to differentiate between different types of parenthetical remarks, such as a side comment versus an explanation or translation, or even parenthetical remarks coming from two different narrators in a passage, braces could serve as an alternative to some of the parentheses.

[13.3] Brackets/square brackets

Brackets have a few uses in fiction both as alternatives to parentheses and for a few special applications.

[13.3.1] Brackets with nested parentheses

The CMOS recommends using brackets to include a parenthetical remark inside another parenthetical remark, instead of nesting parentheses. Here's a reworked example from above.

I first met Barclay Stevens by accident (more like a multi-car-pileup kind of accident) and our encounter was far from pleasant (he was an asshole [the asshole of assholes]).

[13.3.2] Brackets for non-parenthetical comments

Whereas parentheses are used to add information or remarks to the sentence, brackets serve to add material or a comment that would normally *not* be part of the sentence or narrative. What if you're quoting a passage of Shakespeare and you suspect your readers won't know the meaning of some word or phrase in the quote? Brackets can serve to differentiate the explanation from a simple parenthetical remark.

> The first line of Act I of *Romeo and Juliet* opens with Sampson and Gregory, armed with swords. Sampson utters the line "Gregory, o' my word, we'll not carry coals [put up with affronts]." Readers might not know what "coals" means. Brackets provide a way to insert that information.

Use brackets to add the translation of a foreign word or phrase for the reader and to make it stand out more than parentheses would.

> "It is not polite to ask a woman her age," Sophie said in her lovely French accent. "Only because you are *jeune et très beau* [young and handsome] will I tell you."

Brackets can be used to clarify information in quotations, particularly when they are taken out of full context, as when a news report is quoting something in part. News reporters often do this to clarify points for their readers. In a novel, a character might be talking to the police or a reporter in one scene, and later read the newspaper account.

> [ORIGINAL] "As I told the police," Mark said to the reporter, "I got there at six, to discuss our parents' will. I rang the doorbell, but nobody answered. The door was unlocked. I went inside and found it in the living room."

> [QUOTED AND CLARIFIED] The newspaper reported the story: "The deceased's brother, Mark Lamont, said in a brief interview, 'I got [to my sister's house] at six [p.m.], to discuss our parents' latest will. I rang the doorbell, but nobody answered. The door was unlocked. I went inside and found [her body] in the living room.' According to the medical examiner's report, his sister had been shot three hours prior."

[13.3.3] Brackets to emphasize side comments

If you're writing a story where you need to pop out of the narrator's head to offer information or insight beyond a simple parenthetical, then brackets offer an option.

Let's say you're writing a story where two narrators are collaborating and their viewpoints alternate, but they cross-comment during the narration. Our example deliberately overuses the technique for illustration purposes. We also italicized the comments (an option) to make them stand out. The two characters here are Jake and Scott.

Jake got a part-time faculty position at the University of Colorado to conceal his covert activities and to provide him with a legitimate means of inflicting mental anguish on students. [JAKE: *Students are supposed to suffer mental anguish. It's their lot in life.*] He suggested that I apply to grad school to keep myself out of trouble. [JAKE: *And away from the druggies.*] [SCOTT: *I don't do drugs.*] [JAKE: *See, my plan worked.*] I was accepted into the Biochemistry program for the following spring.

[13.3.4] Brackets to insert external sounds or actions

Brackets can be used to show sounds or actions going on around the character when it would otherwise be difficult to show these in a smooth manner.

Anderson darted across the street through the gridlocked traffic [horns blared], fleeing his would-be killer. He leaped onto the hood of one car ["hey, asshole!"] and back down to the street a second before a bullet whizzed past his ear.

[13.3.5] Brackets with the Latin "sic"

The Latin word *sic* means "so, thus" and it's frequently enclosed in brackets [sic] in a text to indicate that an apparent error was intentional or part of the original. While few writers will employ this in fiction, here's one example where it might be used.

Terry retyped the letter exactly as he'd gotten it from his father. Devon sat next to him as a witness and would notarize the typed copy, a precaution in case the original didn't reach its destination: "If your [sic] reading this, I'm dead and you have to go on without me."

CHAPTER FOURTEEN

ITALICS AND EMPHASIS

[14.1] Italics basics

Although technically not a mark of punctuation, italics (or italic type) nevertheless serve to set off and clarify like other punctuation.

NOTE: "italics" a plural noun, requiring a plural verb ("italics are" not "italics is").

Italic type functions to highlight or emphasize text for a variety of purposes. In this chapter we're going to show those and discuss other methods of emphasis as well.

We've previously discussed italics vs. quotation marks for designating titles, but we'll repeat those in [14.3].

[14.2] Italics for emphasis

Use italics to emphasize words when emphasis is required, but not when it's obvious the emphasis is already there or when it is indicated by an exclamation mark or one of the other techniques listed later in this chapter. Don't double up on emphasis.

In dialogue or a character's thoughts when you need to emphasize or stress a word or phrase, italicize it. In dialogue, consider whether it's better to emphasize a word or words (italics) instead of using an exclamation for the whole sentence.

"What are you doing here?" she asked.

"What are *you* doing here?" she asked.

Alicia pointed a finger at Rob. "Don't even *think* about it."

What was this guy all about, and why was *I* trusting *him*?

"Say it anyway you want, but you lied to me!" (The whole sentence is shouted.)

"Say it anyway you want, but *you lied to me*." (Only the italicized part is shouted.)

[14.3] Other uses of italics

[14.3.1] Italics with titles

Book titles: both fiction and nonfiction

Magazines: *Newsweek, National Geographic*

Newspapers: *The Chicago Tribune, The New York Times*

Plays and musicals: *Our Town, Hamlet, Camelot*

Long poems: *The Odyssey, Paradise Lost*

Movies/motion pictures: *Gone With The Wind, Star Wars*

Television shows: *I Love Lucy, NCIS, The Price Is Right*

Operas: *Madame Butterfly, Carmen*

Ships, trains, and aircraft: *The Queen Mary, Motor City Special, The Spruce Goose*

NOTES: In some cases "the" in front of newspapers and the names of ships, trains, and aircraft is not italicized. The location of the newspaper may be shown in normal type: Chicago *Tribune*. Newspapers and other publications rarely italicize the names of other newspapers and publications, so you have some liberty.

[14.3.2] Italics in scientific names

For the scientific name of genus and species, the proper format is to capitalize the genus, use lowercase for the species, and render both in italics.

Canis familiaris (the common dog)

Solanum lycopersicum (tomato)

Equus caballus (horse)

[14.3.3] Italics with foreign words and phrases

Foreign language words and phrases (including when your characters speak in another language) are italicized except for those common words that have come into everyday use.

Zeitgeist, ad nauseam

"*Yo hablo inglés*," Juan said.

"*Je parle anglais*," Jacques told me, saying he spoke English so he wouldn't have to listen to me butcher the French language.

"*Wie heisst du?*... Vaht is your name?" Wolfgang asked him, pronouncing the English *w* like a *v*.

Do not italicize common and familiar foreign words.

> ad infinitum, bona fide, bon voyage, carte blanche, en route, et cetera, ex officio, gratis, hors d'oeuvre, kaput (kaputt in German), poltergeist, risqué, vice versa

If these words are being spoken in their original language, italicize the entire foreign line.

> In her apartment, I spotted what appeared to be a rather spicy romance novel on her coffee table and figured impressing her with my hopefully passable French couldn't hurt my chances. "*Ce livre est un peu risqué, n'cest-ce pas?*" She smiled at me.

Here are the two CMOS guidelines for italicizing foreign words:

(1) Use italics for foreign words and phrases that are likely to be unfamiliar to readers. Familiar foreign words and phrases and those listed in M-W should not be italicized. If you feel it's likely not familiar to your readers anyway, you may italicize it. Also italicize if you want to call attention to it. (e.g., *sotto voce* and *verboten* are in M-W, but some readers may not know these.)

(2) If a foreign word is used repeatedly in your story such that it becomes familiar, you need to italicize only the first time it's used. If the word is used rarely in the story, italicize throughout.

When you use foreign words that have special accent marks, retain those marks in your writing unless the word has become common enough in English that the marks are dropped. In the list of foreign words below, the version in parentheses is no longer necessary in modern English usage, although it's not incorrect. Do not italicize these words in any case.

> naive (naïve), facade (façade), cafe (café)

Because of possible confusion with *resume* (to continue), *résumé* (a list of your job qualifications) should be written with the accents. "Sauté" retains the accent. (See [16.1] for how to enter accented letters.)

[14.3.5] Italics to highlight a word or phrase

You may highlight something to distinguish it from the rest of the sentence. This is different from italicizing for emphasis. Quote marks are also acceptable in this case.

My brother loves to use big words. *Mendacity*, meaning *a tendency to tell lies*, is his current favorite.

My brother loves to use big words. "Mendacity," meaning "a tendency to tell lies," is his current favorite.

Truth in advertising is a principle that all businesses should follow.

When he asked her what her biggest problem was, she said *weight*, but he thought she had said *wait* so she could think about it.

James is a person who makes sure he's dotted all his *i*'s and crossed all his *t*'s. (In this case, only the letter, not the *'s* should be italicized.)

[14.3.6] Italics to indicate a character's direct thoughts

It is standard practice to italicize direct thoughts, that is, those words that would be in quotation marks if spoken out loud. Because quotes are generally reserved for actual spoken words, it's wise not to put such thoughts in quotes to avoid confusion. (See [14.5])

Adrian went inside and was about to remove his jacket when he noticed a light in the library. Eli was home. Unfortunately. *Might as well get this over with.*

Drake hated relying on someone else for a ride—*especially these pot-smoking losers*—but his parents had left for the weekend and he sure as hell wasn't going to stay home. *Screw it all! The 'rents are away, Drake's gonna play.* He stuck his hands in his pockets and walked toward Greg's car.

Indirect thoughts are not italicized. We'll cover thoughts in detail in [14.5].

[14.3.7] Italics to show Sign Language conversations

While Sign Language is likely not something you'll commonly use in your writing, but if you do, you may wish to make it stand out from other dialogue. (See [15.8.5] for our ideas on how to do this.)

[14.3.8] Italics to show something being read

When a character is reading something (a letter or book), either to himself or out loud, italics can be used to set the passage apart from the rest of the narrative.

He placed the journal on the desk, sat, and began to read:

How I came to be here is a long tale, but I seem to have all the time in this world to write it. I don't know how long I will be here or if escape is possible. I may die here.

Use italics sparingly for this purpose because long passages of italic type are more difficult to read. Nevertheless, this is a standard practice in fiction, and such passages stand out well so that the reader has little doubt as to the intent. Bold type should not be used except for very short passages because it's visually more distracting than italic type.

When it's necessary to use many italicized passages throughout a work (letters or journal passages that a character is reading periodically), keep them short or present them as a separate scene or chapter with appropriate transitions. If you put such passages in separate scenes or chapters, you can avoid the need for italics by letting the reader know what it is with a note or scene heading.

[14.4] Italics within italicized passages

When a passage is already italicized and you want to use italics within that passage, un-italicize the affected words.

Jeff looked at his bank balance then read the note from the blackmailer again. *How am* I *supposed to raise* ten thousand dollars *in twenty-four hours?*

Her letter read: *Dear Kevin, I'm sorry it didn't work out between us. I like you very much, as a friend, but I don't* love *you.*

On that Friday afternoon, Paul very much regretted his habitual procrastination. *How am I supposed to read all of* Huck Finn *and do a three-thousand-word book report by* Monday?

* * *

ADVANCED: ITALICS AND EMPHASIS

[14.5] Dealing with character thoughts

[14.5.1] Options for expressing thoughts

Three basic methods exist for showing a character's thoughts: simple exposition, direct thoughts (the actual words the character is thinking), and indirect thoughts (mental musings). A longstanding convention uses italics to show direct thoughts in fiction.

[EXPOSITION] Gary scanned the alley, looking for his adversary. He wondered how Jackson had disappeared so quickly.

[INDIRECT THOUGHTS] Gary scanned the alley, looking for his adversary. How had Jackson disappeared so quickly?

[DIRECT THOUGHTS] Gary scanned the alley, looking for his adversary. *How did Jackson disappear so quickly?*

The first is telling what Gary thought. The second is showing Gary thinking. The third gives his actual thoughts, which is also showing. Notice the verb tenses used. Direct thoughts are expressed in the present or simple past tense, whereas indirect thoughts are expressed in past or past perfect. Here are more examples.

[EXPOSITION] Clutch in, Craig revved the engine before shutting it off. He believed that people who owned a Vette were morally obligated to show it off.

[INDIRECT]

Clutch in, Craig revved the engine before shutting it off. When you owned a Vette, you were morally obligated to show it off.

169

Unseen, Robin listened to the other cheerleaders plotting to make her look bad. She'd show them. She'd show them all!

[DIRECT]

Clutch in, Craig revved the engine before shutting it off. *When you own a Vette, you're morally obligated to show it off.*

Unseen, Robin listened to the other cheerleaders plotting to make her look bad. *I'll show them. I'll show them all!*

Although some writers put thoughts in quotation marks as either normal or italic text, this practice can make it difficult for a reader to distinguish between thoughts and spoken dialogue. Most authoritics agree that quotation marks should be reserved for spoken words.

However, the CMOS says, "Thoughts, imagined dialogue, and other interior discourse may be enclosed in quotation marks or not, according to the context or the writer's preference."

Some writers (more common in literary works) use neither italics nor quotes. They use tags (such as "he thought") to indicate thoughts. This is a style preference in the same vein as not using quotation marks for direct dialogue.

Section [15.8.4] deals with telepathic communication and projected thoughts.

[14.5.2] Tags for thoughts

We see thought tags used in published novels all the time. To our way of thinking, this is done because the writer doesn't trust the reader to understand that it's a thought. If you craft your prose properly, such tags are usually unnecessary, especially if you use italics for direct thoughts.

Sometimes a tag may be necessary to make clear that something is a thought, as opposed to simple emphasis, or to clarify the thinker. If you're unsure, ask yourself whether the intent is clear, or can be made clear, without the tag. Where you do need to use such a tag, punctuate it the same way that you would for dialogue (with a comma, or a ? or ! replacing a comma).

The following are "not recommended," but note the punctuation with the tags used.

Gary scanned the alley, looking for his adversary. How had Jackson disappeared so quickly? he wondered. ("he wondered" is redundant.)

Gary scanned the alley, looking for his adversary. How did Jackson disappear so quickly? he thought. (tag is unnecessary)

Gary scanned the alley, looking for his adversary. *"How did Jackson disappear so quickly?"* (use quote marks or italics, not both)

Clutch in, he revved the engine before shutting it off. *When you own a Vette, you're morally obligated to show it off,* Craig thought. (change the "he" to "Craig" and tag is not needed)

[14.6] Other methods of emphasis

In addition to italic type, there exist three other basic ways to emphasize something: the exclamation mark, boldface type, and all capital letters (all caps).

[14.6.1] The exclamation mark

The exclamation mark can be used after an individual word or phrase, especially when that is isolated with parentheses or a dash. This use is not common today. We gave examples in [4.6.3].

Joe watched his brother launch himself from the diving board and—he couldn't believe it!—make a *triple* somersault before landing in the water.

The horse I bet on to win came in second (damn!) by less than a length.

[14.6.2] Boldface type

Boldface type is rarely used in fiction other than for titles. Unless there is a very compelling reason to use boldface type, we recommend not using it in fiction.

[14.6.3] Use of all capital letters

Words in all caps indicate shouting when used in dialogue. This can single out a particular word or phrase and stress it more than an exclamation mark would. You can use this in combination with exclamation marks and italics to show an escalating situation.

> "Out of the question."
> "We'll be careful."
> "No! It's far too dangerous."
> "If we don't, Greg will *die!*"
> "I said *NO!*"
> "But—"
> "*ABSOLUTELY NOT!*..." Mack sat, bowed his head, and took deep breaths. "You don't understand...." He looked up and shook his head. "If you go in there, we *all* die."

In his novel *A Prayer for Owen Meany*, author John Irving used ALL CAPS for Owen's speech because Owen was "a boy with a wrecked voice." This was Irving's way to keep the reader reminded of that. Owen isn't the main character, so the technique works because Irving does not litter every page with that dialogue. It also rendered dialogue tags largely unnecessary for Owen's character.

[14.6.4] More options for emphasis

Throughout this book we've seen how sentence fragments can add emphasis. Here's an example that also employs hyphens and ellipses with fragments to add strong pauses. The hyphen lets us stress the syllables.

> "You didn't call Rudy like I told you!" Greg said to Nate.
> "Yes. I. Did."
> "Well, he isn't here."
> Nate turned and headed toward the door. "Not... my... prob-lem."

CHAPTER FIFTEEN

PUNCTUATING DIALOGUE

Throughout this book (and in chapter 12), we have shown and discussed how to punctuate dialogue, but dialogue is such an important aspect of fiction that we wanted to bring it all together in a separate chapter along with additional details and techniques.

[15.1] Conventions for writing dialogue

[15.1.1] Put dialogue inside quotation marks

Direct dialogue (dialogue spoken, as opposed to reported) is normally put inside quotation marks: double quotes in American English and single (or double) in UK English. Indirect dialogue is not put in quotes. (See [15.7] for alternatives to quotation marks.)

[DIRECT] "I have no idea what that means," he said.

[INDIRECT] He said he had no idea what that means.

[15.1.2] Position of other punctuation

In US English, most punctuation associated with the dialogue falls inside the quote marks (comma, period, question mark, exclamation mark, ellipsis, and the dash). The semicolon and colon go outside the quote marks, but these are rare at the end of dialogue lines.

Eli Howard knocked on the door of Adam's room, his ruse in place.
"Who is it?" the voice on the other side asked.
"Cyrus Hayes sent me."
With his vampire telepathy, Eli knew Adam was peering back at him.
"Hayes didn't mention anyone was coming, Mister..."
"Radley."
Adam hesitated.
"My company made those special eye drops," Eli said.
Adam opened the door. His eyes widened at seeing Eli. "I expected—"
"A white man? That is statistically unlikely in Detroit."

NOTE: In UK English most punctuation goes outside the quote marks in dialogue unless the punctuation in question is part of the quoted material. Refer to the appropriate style guides for UK usage.

[15.1.3] Capitalize the first word of dialogue lines

The beginning word of a dialogue line is always capitalized, regardless of where it falls in a sentence. (See the exceptions under [15.3] for interrupted and continued dialogue.)

[15.1.4] New paragraph when speaker changes

By convention, whenever the speaker changes, you should start a new paragraph. Putting the dialogue of two different speakers in one paragraph can be confusing to a reader. (See [15.5])

Within any paragraph that contains dialogue, it's best to include *only* those words, actions, observations, and thoughts that apply to that particular speaker. This helps avoid confusion and minimizes the need for dialogue tags.

NOTE: In dialogue passages, readers usually assume that a new paragraph indicates a new speaker, but sometimes it's necessary to extend the dialogue of one speaker over several paragraphs. (See [15.4]) Note carefully the three passages below.

[CLEAR]

Val Radley stood and came around her desk as the security guard escorted the dark-suited FBI agent into her office.

The agent proffered his hand. "I'm Calvin Jacobs, the lead investigator in this case, Mrs. Radley." He hesitated. "I'll try to make this as easy as I can for you."

She shook his hand. "I appreciate that, Mr. Jacobs." She indicated the two chairs in front of the desk. "Please, make yourself comfortable." Even though she wasn't.

=====

[AWKWARD AND CONFUSING]

Val Radley stood and came around her desk as the security guard escorted the dark-suited FBI agent into her office. The agent proffered his hand. "I'm Calvin Jacobs, the lead investigator in this case, Mrs. Radley." He hesitated. "I'll try to

174

make this as easy as I can for you." She shook his hand. "I appreciate that, Mr. Jacobs." She indicated the two chairs in front of the desk. "Please, make yourself comfortable." Even though she wasn't.

[CONFUSING (as to who is speaking)]

Val Radley stood and came around her desk as the security guard escorted the dark-suited FBI agent into her office.

The agent proffered his hand.

"I'm Calvin Jacobs, the lead investigator in this case, Mrs. Radley."

He hesitated.

"I'll try to make this as easy as I can for you."

She shook his hand.

"I appreciate that, Mr. Jacobs."

She indicated the two chairs in front of the desk.

"Please, make yourself comfortable."

Even though she wasn't.

[15.1.5] Dialogue tags

A dialogue tag is a speech attribute that tells who spoke the line and perhaps how the words were delivered. It may be placed anywhere in the line. It may precede the line, but more often follows if the line is short. For longer passages, the tag is often placed after the first sentence or close to the beginning of the dialogue line.

Whether a dialogue tag precedes, follows, or splits the dialog, a comma is used to separate it from the spoken words. When the dialogue before the tag is a question or exclamation, a ? or ! *replaces* the comma. This is why we mentioned in chapter 4 that these two marks sometimes substitute for a comma. In dialogue, these punctuation marks are clarifiers, not sentence terminators. They do not mark the end of the sentence if a tag follows.

Dialogue tags are never capitalized unless they begin the sentence or the tag begins with a word that is normally capitalized. They are considered part of the sentence, which is also why a comma (not a period) separates the tag from the dialogue.

[CORRECT]

"I can't go tonight," Paul said.

Jessica asked, "Who else is coming with us?"

"I have better things to do than to watch you get drunk!" he said.

"Can I bring a friend?" she asked.

"I'm going to the prom with Vince," she said. "You can go by yourself for all I care."

[INCORRECT]

"I can't go to the party with you tonight." She said.

"I have better things to do than to watch you get drunk!" He said.

"Can I bring a friend?" She asked.

If you remember that the tag is part of the sentence, then you'll remember not to capitalize the tag unless it begins the sentence.

Cyrus Hayes stood beside Eli in the middle of the street, one hand braced on the sword whose point rested on the ground. "This could be a blessing for us," he said.

An incredulous Eli asked, "How is this a blessing?"

"How is it *not* a blessing? We don't have to kill them ourselves," Cyrus replied. Abruptly, he pivoted, sword point inches away from the belly of the villager behind them.

The man raised his hands. "Please don't kill me!" he said in German.

Eli put his hand on Cyrus' wrist. "There has been enough death here."

"Apparently he doesn't think so or he would not have snuck up on us with a knife."

[15.2] Dialogue tag details

The purpose of dialogue tags is to help readers keep track of the speaker. Period. Using them for any other purpose may weaken your writing.

[15.2.1] Format of dialogue tags

The currently accepted practice in US English is to place the speaker's name or pronoun in front of the verb (John said, he said).

UK usage may differ. Older writing sometimes inverts these (said John, said the old man). It's even rarer for a pronoun to follow the verb (said he, said I). However, it's acceptable when the tone and style dictate it. Note the tone in each of these examples:

> With a gleam in his eye, William said, "I know exactly how we can do it."

> "Count me in," I replied.

> "The danger is exceedingly great," said Joram gravely, "but great riches and potent magicks are locked within Lord Basil's treasure house."

> "We must make our plan with care," said I. "Lord Basil's High Mage has summoned fell creatures to serve as his guards.

[15.2.2] Placement of dialogue tags

Dialogue tags can occur anywhere in the dialogue passage. How you punctuate these depends on the sentence, but the tag is part of the sentence, not separate from it. When the tag introduces the line, it calls more attention to itself, which is fine if that's what you want. Most of the time you want dialogue tags to be as unobtrusive as possible.

If the dialogue is more than one or two sentences, or if the sentences are long, putting the tag closer to the front tells the reader sooner who is speaking and avoids confusion when multiple people are talking. The following are all acceptable, but note the differences in feel and delivery of the lines.

> "I really don't care," Craig said, "if you go. That's not my problem."

> "I really don't care if you go," Craig said. "That's not my problem."

> "I really don't care if you go. That's not my problem," Craig said.

> Craig said, "I really don't care if you go. That's not my problem."

> "I really don't care if you go. That's not my problem. You're old enough to make your own decisions and free to do whatever your little heart desires," Craig said.

"I really don't care if you go," Craig said. "That's not my problem. You're old enough to make your own decisions and free to do whatever your little heart desires."

[15.2.3] What should a dialogue tag include?

A dialogue tag should not be an information dump. Its job is to tell who is speaking. If the tag draws attention away from the dialogue, it's going beyond its job description and not in a good way. The standard tag is *said* for a statement and *said* or *asked* for a question. These words largely invisible to the reader and not intrusive unless you overuse tags in general.

Other common tag words include *answered, cried, inquired, lied, mumbled muttered, questioned, replied, screamed, shouted, spoke, replied, told, whispered, shouted, yelled.* Avoid the temptation to use non-*said* words except when necessary. Doing so tells the reader that you are trying too hard with your dialogue.

Some beginning writers think they must be specific with tags and use words such as *admitted, agreed, argued, barked, begged, bragged, demanded, interrupted, mentioned, nagged, pleaded, remembered, requested, threatened, warned, wondered.* This often leads to weak writing that can sound amateurish.

Good dialogue should show these *in the dialogue*. In the following examples, the tag repeats what the dialogue has already told us. This looks amateurish. Using *said* would give a cleaner presentation.

[POOR WRITING, UNNECESSARY TAGS]

"You're right," he admitted.

"By the way, I'm going out tonight," she informed.

"*Please*, may I go with you?" she begged.

"When we were young, Dad took us to the movies every Saturday," she recalled.

"Put down the knife now, or I swear I will shoot you!" he warned, pointing the gun.

Tags may include additional information or clarifying attributes: *said loudly; spoke with authority; told pointedly; asked tentatively; said as he turned around; whispered, pointing straight ahead.* Use these sparingly for the reasons given previously.

She said tightly, quietly, "Like. Hell. You. Are." (Placing a strong tag first in this case lets the reader anticipate the dialogue.)

[15.2.4] Separate tags and actions

It's better to separate tags and actions because you can often eliminate the need for a tag and craft stronger prose. This will also help to avoid overusing present participles and "said as he..." constructions that we pointed out in chapter 3.

[WEAK] "Put down the knife now, or I swear I will shoot you!" he said as he thrust the gun forward.

[STRONG] He thrust the gun forward. "Put down the knife now, or I swear I will shoot you!"

[15.2.5] Avoid "telling" words in tags

If you need clarifying words, then you may not be doing your job as a writer. After a while, too many non-*said* words begin to stick out. They can distract. Which of the two following passages is stronger and smoother?

[1] "Do you honestly believe those interested in keeping crime and their drug trade alive will let you terminate their activities?" Ling pointed out. "Where whole governments have failed, you expect to succeed?"
"I thought you, out of all of us, would understand," Eli replied.
"I do, Eli, but the odds are not in our favor," she reminded him. "If one sleepless night has you this haggard, I don't want to see you when you fail in this endeavor," she added.
"I'm that bad?" he inquired.
"Tonight you are not a handsome man," she admitted.

=====

[2] "Do you honestly believe those interested in keeping crime and their drug trade alive will let you terminate their activities?" Ling said. "Where whole governments have failed, you expect to succeed?"
"I thought you, out of all of us, would understand," Eli said.

"I do, Eli, but the odds are not in our favor. If one sleepless night has you this haggard, I don't want to see you when you fail in this endeavor."

"I'm that bad?"

"Tonight you are not a handsome man."

A non-*said* word is beneficial when the line can't say it or can't say it without being awkward.

"I can't go out tonight, Chet. I have to study for the math test tomorrow," Kathy said.

Chet flashed his winning smile. "C'mon, Kath. You know it's gonna be a great party."

"You've got a B-average; you don't have to worry," she reminded him. "I'm borderline failing."

=====

Dyson handed him the gun. "You will need this when the battle begins."

"Battle?" he said.

"And keep it concealed so we don't alert them," Dyson told him.

"Battle?" he repeated.

=====

As they snuck closer to the house, Henry nearly stepped on a trap. Frank yanked him back. "Be careful!" Frank whispered.

[15.2.6] Incorrect tag words

Dialogue tag words should be speech attributes, not actions or sounds. We see writers using improper words in tags: *cough, choke, chuckle, giggle, grin, groan, laugh, moan, shrug, sigh, smile, snarl, snicker, sob, whine, wink.* These are sounds or actions, not ways to speak words. How do you laugh, smile, shrug, or wink words? Put such actions into separate sentences.

[CORRECT]

Sandi chuckled at them. "Only you two could have pulled that off."

"I'm sure we'll figure out a way." Dave smiled. "We're smart guys."

She sobbed uncontrollably. "H-he w-was g-going to kill me."

180

"Raise your hands real slow," he said pointing the gun, "and don't try anything stupid."

She laughed. "I think that's funny."

He nearly choked when she told him she'd gotten an F on the math exam. "But you... *never* fail!"

"Just because I don't have fangs doesn't mean I can't be a vampire." He smiled broadly to show he wasn't lying—not about the fangs anyway.

[INCORRECT]

Edwin grinned, "I am pretty awesome, aren't I?" (You can't grin words. Put a period after "grinned")

Josh peeked around the corner and saw Ben and Lisa kissing passionately, "Caught you." He winked at Ben, "I told you she was the one." (use periods, no commas)

"I think that's funny," she laughed. (period, no comma)

"But you... *never* fail," he choked when she told him she'd gotten an F on the math exam. (period, no comma)

"Well, there goes your boyfriend with his latest conquest," Simon snickered." (period, no comma)

"Stop right there!" he hissed. (He hissed, a new sentence)

Some might argue that "hiss" is a legitimate dialogue tag. It can be, but *only* one when limited to a word or a phrase that could be delivered with a hissing sound:

"Ss-stop!" he hissed.

"Because I ss-said ss-so," he hissed.

[15.3] Punctuating interrupted dialogue

A line of dialogue may be interrupted in several ways and may or may not be continued after the break. The punctuation and its placement depend on the nature of the line and the break.

The CMOS says, "Ellipsis may suggest faltering, fragmented speech accompanied by confusion or insecurity." Use ellipses when the speaker is not interrupted by an outside source and naturally pauses or trails off, perhaps waiting for a response or collecting his thoughts.

When an outside source interrupts the speaker, dashes are the preferred punctuation. (See [5.3.4])

[15.3.1] Speaker uncertain or waits for a response

After hearing the King's proposition, the man said, "Your majesty, if I may speak frankly..."
The King nodded.
"I would rather suffer a lifetime in prison than agree to wed your daughter."

=====

"And you did not tell me about this earlier because..."
"Judgment call. I figured if you thought it was taken care of, you'd concentrate more on the mission."

[15.3.2] Halting or nervous speech

For a moment, Ben appreciated Seth's rambling because it took his mind off why he'd come here. "Seth..." Ben swallowed. "I want..." He exhaled, feeling the emotion rising again. "I need... your help." He heard the nervousness in his own voice.

=====

A woman came up to them. "Madam Sophie, is he your new servant?"
Joseph avoided looking at the woman's bare breasts.
"He will serve me," Sophie said. She took hold of his chin and turned his head back at the woman. "Do you not like what you see?"
"She is..."
"Naked? Yes. What is wrong with a beautiful, naked woman?"

[15.3.3] Continuing speech after an ellipsis break

What we mean here is that the dialogue ends with an ellipsis and something intervenes before the dialogue continues. These are more challenging situations where multiple options exist. The CMOS, provides incomplete guidance here. We therefore propose guidelines for five cases [15.3.3.1-5] of interrupted dialogue and we include our rationale for each case based on the established uses of ellipses and reasonable extensions of those.

[15.3.3.1] Ellipsis ends a complete sentence

When an ellipsis ends a sentence and we want to show that the speaker will continue after he pauses, use *four* dots to end the sentence. The first is the period and the ellipsis dots follow it.

RATIONALE: Although the sentence is complete, we use four dots to differentiate this from an incomplete sentence that continues after the ellipsis.

> Jensen studied each of us. "I... don't know if we can pull this off...." He pressed both hands behind his neck, massaging it, and looked at the ground then up at the sky before he focused on us again. "I don't see that we have another option."

[15.3.3.2] Unfinished sentence continues after a break

When the dialogue continues after intervening narrative (tag, phrase, or sentence), the situation is more complicated with handling the ellipsis points. We could find no unanimous agreement, so we present three options and our rationale for each. The choice is yours. Employ the one that seems best in your situation, but be consistent with whichever one you select.

[OPTION 1] Continue the dialogue after the break as if the break were *not* there. The ellipsis is *not* repeated to introduce to the continuation.

RATIONALE: Unlike dashes, ellipses occur singly, not in pairs.

> Jason poked a finger at David. "How about *you* get in line and save us a spot while we park the car so we can all get into the club faster? See ya in a few..." He coughed out a barely audible "hours."

Here we treated the "See ya in a few" as an unfinished sentence and broke it with an ellipsis. We finished off with a new sentence. We did *not* treat "he coughed out a barely audible" as a dialogue tag because it's not a tag. We can view "hours" either as continued dialogue or as a word in scare quotes.

"It is not *my* experiment. It is *our* experiment, one that will benefit every vampire, especially young ones. I will personally supervise the execution..." He smiled at his choice of words. "of the experiments."

Here, a full sentence intervenes, but we treated it as continued dialogue and didn't capitalize the following line.

[OPTION 2] Use an ellipsis to introduce the continued dialogue after the break.

RATIONALE: When using ellipses for text omissions between paragraphs, the CMOS shows an ellipsis at the end of one paragraph *and* at the start of the next paragraph. While this is not shown for dialogue, we can extend its use for dialogue.

"It is not *my* experiment. It is *our* experiment, one that will benefit every vampire, especially young ones. I will personally supervise the execution..." He smiled at his choice of words. "...of the experiments."

"Now, I bet you wanna know why I was in *this* room," Drake told the guard, who nodded and raised his eyebrows at the same time. "Well, it's a room where almost no one goes, and I figured it was a good place to call my..." Drake did the quote thing with his fingers as he said, "...*friend* to say what a nice time I had with her last night."

[OPTION 3] Set off the interrupting passage with dashes instead of ellipses.

RATIONALE: Dashes are used in non-dialogue to set off both short and long interrupting passages. We have observed authors doing it this way. If you treat the interruption as a parenthetical element, an action that accompanies the dialogue, then dashes can be justified. Note that there are no spaces before or after the dashes.

"It is not *my* experiment. It is *our* experiment, one that will benefit every vampire, especially young ones. I will personally supervise the execution"—he smiled at his choice of words—"of the experiments."

But when the interrupting passage is long, ellipses may look better than dashes.

184

"We are in quadrant six, Castill system," he said. "That..." He pointed to a strain-to-see, blue flicker of light thirty degrees above the northern horizon and on the verge of being consumed by the advancing clouds. "...is Ranor."

[15.3.3.3] Use of ? or ! with ellipsis

When a complete sentence or fragment *before* an ellipsis requires a question mark or exclamation mark, the ellipsis follows it.

If the sentence or fragment is *unfinished* and is clearly an exclamation or a question, the ellipsis precedes the question mark or exclamation mark.

When his mother asked if he'd had any strange dreams lately, Charlie quickly replied, "No!... No dreams at all."

"Seriously? That's the most idiotic...!

"Oh, my!" her mother said, seeing the mess. "What happened here?... And where is your sister?"

=====

> "Why didn't you tell me sooner?" Seth said. "He *is* my nephew. I could have been there for you."
> Ben tilted his head up. "Can you help him?"
> "How...?" Realization crept into Seth's expression. "You want me to... change him? Into a vampire?"

[15.3.3.4] Comma with ellipsis

A comma normally separates the dialogue from its tag, but if a tag follows an ellipsis, an *optional* comma may follow the ellipsis.

The CMOS uses the comma, but some argue that it's unnecessary or that it looks strange. Since a comma separating the dialogue line from a tag can be replaced by a question mark or exclamation mark, why not by an ellipsis (a separating mark like the comma)? We prefer *no* comma and suspect that few editors would argue.

"But... but...," Tom said. (the CMOS recommendation)

"I don't see how... unless..." Harry said. He rubbed his chin and narrowed his eyes the way he always did just before he was about to say something brilliant. (our preference, no comma)

185

EXCEPTION: When the word before the ellipsis is a vocative (direct address), a comma is needed to clarify the vocative, but note the position of the comma in these examples.

"Mr. Brewer,..." Stefan decided to dispense with formality. "Ben,... you made a difficult decision, and I know it was not an easy one."

"Ken,..." Sam said, not knowing how to begin.

[15.3.3.5] Ellipsis to introduce dialogue

Use an ellipsis to begin a dialogue line that starts somewhere in the middle, such as a piece of an overheard conversation. We recommend *no* space between the ellipsis and the first word so you don't risk stranding the ellipsis at the end of the previous line.

Jessica carefully picked up the extension phone and listened. "*...to be there sometime tomorrow.*"

Aaron snuck up next to the cracked-open door. "...will take care of it. Aaron Foster won't be alive after tomorrow."

He switched to a weather channel. "...expect periods of heavy snow tomorrow.

[15.3.4] Continuing speech after speaker is interrupted

When the speaker is interrupted, whether by another speaker or an external event, the dash is used to show such an interruption. If the speaker continues after the interruption, a dash introduces the continuation (dashes occur in pairs like most commas). Use a dash if the interrupting speaker continues the first speaker's dialogue.

"I guess I'll help," Adrian told her. "Drake wants to help, too."
"You must protect him," she said. He's the age you were when—"
"—when I made a bad decision."

=====

"Malcolm assigned me to you to accommodate your—" Dmitri said.
"He doesn't trust me," Erik said.
"It's not that. He figured you'd feel more at ease—"

186

"So I don't think Malcolm is manipulating me, you mean."

"—more at ease because I'm human like you. He's merely looking out for your interests."

"And I should trust you because you're not a vampire."

Dmitri smiled. "I would."

=====

"I'm gonna ride my bike over to Chrissy's," Kate said. "Oh, wait. Her parents and her—"

"Her parents and *she*," her sister said.

"What?... Well, *they* went to Disney World, and the rest of our friends are somewhere besides the middle of nowhere-to-go-and-nothing-to-see Kansas." (we used hyphens instead of single quotes for the long adjective phrase simply to avoid nesting quotes)

=====

The apartment was empty. "Where are they?" Peter asked.

"Whatever happened," Doug said, "we have to—"

The living room window shattered behind him.

Doug spun around. "What the—" was all he managed before he vanished in a flash of light, leaving Peter gaping.

[15.3.5] A tag splits the sentence

If the sentence is merely broken up into two parts with no pauses or interruptions, use the commas, as if the tag fell at the start or end of the line.

"Let's go for a walk," Eli said to him, "just you and me."

"Where do you think," I asked, "this road goes?"

"I'm not so sure," he said, shaking his head, "that your way is a good idea."

* * *

ADVANCED: PUNCTUATING DIALOGUE

[15.4] Multiple paragraphs for one speaker

When dialogue extends over multiple paragraphs, use open quotes at the start of the first paragraph and to begin each successive paragraph. As long as the dialogue (or quoted material) continues uninterrupted by tags or other non-dialogue, do not insert a close quote until the dialogue ends. In this example, paragraphs two and three have no close quote.

"I don't understand," Jake said.

"While an organism is alive, the carbon-14 ratio in its body maintains an equilibrium with the environment," Bryce said. "After it dies, the radioactive decay takes over. Every 5700 years, half of the C-14 decays.

"Any organic material should have a C-14 content equal to or less than what's in the carbon dioxide in the atmosphere. If it's greater, then either the lab screwed up—but they said they ran it three times to be sure they hadn't—or the sample was exposed to radiation. The black stone was not radioactive, and my Geiger counter picked up no radiation around the area.

"After the C-14 results, I took a second bone sample to a biochemist who works with ancient DNA. He said it was more human than anything, but it matched nothing in the databases. Meanwhile, I had given a small piece of the scroll to a forensic chemist I know."

"What scroll?" Jake asked.

Bryce reached into a crevice and pulled out a cylinder six inches long.

[15.5] Multiple speakers in a paragraph

We said previously that, by convention, you should start a new paragraph when the speaker changes [15.1.4]. Sometimes, a writer might want to go against that convention.

For one, it lets you compress the narrative on the page. This might be desirable in some situations, but it should not be your sole reason for doing so.

A more compelling reason is to speed up the narrative pace. Back-and-forth lines in the same paragraph will do this. But you must weigh that against confusing the reader and causing him to slow down or to have to re-read the passage, which negates the speed-up effect you're trying to achieve.

NOTE: Our advice against omitting quotation marks in dialogue or using alternatives to those in [15.7] especially applies here.

We present two examples. The first is conventionally paragraphed [Recommended]. In the second, we've put more than one speaker into some paragraphs [Not recommended]. Both examples use no dialogue tags, which also speeds up the pace, but some may find the passage more challenging to read as a result.

[RECOMMENDED]

The apartment buzzer startled him. Adam went to the door and pressed the intercom button. "Yeah?"

"Special messenger, delivery for Adam Mathews."

"What service you with?"

"Quik Trak."

It sounded like a kid, but voices could be deceptive. No one except Cyrus knew where he lived, and Cyrus always used FedEx.

"What kind of delivery?"

"Not my job to ask."

"How big is the package?"

"Letter size. Hey, I got other deliveries. You want this or not?"

"Leave it."

"It requires a signature."

Adam grunted. "All right." He made sure the gun strapped behind him was accessible then buzzed the guy in.

=====

[NOT RECOMMENDED]

The apartment buzzer startled him. Adam went to the door and pressed the intercom button.

"Yeah?" "Special messenger, delivery for Adam Mathews." "What service you with?" "Quik Trak."

Sounded like a kid, but voices could be deceptive. No one except Cyrus knew where he lived, and Cyrus always used FedEx.

"What kind of delivery?" "Not my job to ask." "How big is the package?" "Letter size. Hey, I got other deliveries. You want this or not?" "Leave it." "It requires a signature."

Adam grunted. "All right." He made sure the gun strapped behind him was accessible then buzzed the guy in.

In the [Not recommended] example, although it is more difficult to read, it does speed up the pace. To help avoid confusion, we used a pattern in the paragraphs: each begins with the first speaker and ends with the second speaker.

TIP: When employing any less-conventional technique such as this, be sure that using it actually serves the narrative.

[15.6] Why punctuate dialogue at all?

Consider the following.

John said I do not need to go to the store. (Ambiguous. Is John saying that *he* doesn't need to go, or is he telling me that *I* don't need to go?)

John said that I do not need to go to the store. (Clear)

John said, "I do not need to go to the store." (Conventional)

John said, I do not need to go to the store. (Dialogue without quote marks. It's clear because of the comma, but less conventional.)

Although we can omit the quotation marks, we can't leave out the comma, not if we want the meaning clear.

[15.7] Alternatives to quotation marks

The *convention* is to use quotation marks around direct speech. Most readers expect this. We've seen enough complaints from American readers about the use of single quotation marks in UK novels to advise caution against abandoning quotation marks.

[15.7.1] Reasons not to use quote marks

We've heard a variety of reasons: The writer doesn't like how quotation marks look in general (James Joyce); the writer prefers minimalist punctuation (Cormac McCarthy); omitting them streamlines the writing and gives it more immediacy; they look ugly in a particular font. But it's your decision to use them or not.

[15.7.2] The quotation dash

Some writers (and some foreign languages) employ the "quotation dash." This is a single dash that introduces a line of dialogue. A passage from James Joyce's short story "The Dead" will illustrate. Joyce insisted on this style, but his publishers did not always follow his wishes.

He walked rapidly towards the door.

—Oh no, sir! cried the girl, following. Really, sir, I wouldn't take it.

—Christmas-time! Christmas-time! said Gabriel, almost trotting to the stairs and waving his hand in her deprecation.

The girl, seeing that he had gained the stairs, called out after him:

—Well, thank you, sir.

[15.7.3] Script format

For writing that has extensive dialogue, one might use older-style movie or play script formatting. We also showed examples of this in [9.6]. Quotation marks are optional with this format, but you may wish to use them for consistency with other dialogue.

Becky: Are you ready for your Literature test tomorrow?
Ken: No problem.
Becky: Was it ever? A problem?
Ken: No.
Becky: That's what I thought.

[15.8] Special cases: other dialogue sources

[15.8.1] Dialogue coming from phones, TV, radios, etc.

Sometimes we have to deal with dialogue coming from audio devices (radio, TV, loudspeaker, speakerphone), or speech heard on a recording. We may wish to distinguish between the dialogue of the characters physically present and that of the non-present voices. Commonly, the dialogue from audio device is shown in italics. Some sources say that the text should not be italicized at all, but we feel that doing so enhances the reader's experience. Using italics this way may eliminate the need for some tags. In this example, it's completely clear who is speaking, without tags after the first one.

"Eric just walked in, Mr. Foster," Sonya said. "I'm putting you on speakerphone."

"Eric, you have acquired the target? Alive, I trust?"

"Yes, sir."

"*Coherent?*"

"In his most impeccable British English."

"*The financial incentive—*"

"Was more than sufficient. he settled for less than half what you authorized."

"*In that case, we will let him live to spend it.*"

[15.8.2] Text & instant messages (IM), computer chats

The writer should choose a format for these that best fits the situation. One option is to treat the dialogue like a script. Because chexmix (his viewpoint) initiates the conversation below, we put his words in normal type and the other person's words in italics, but that's not necessary. We could easily include other people in the conversation without confusion as to who is speaking. Typically such chats use minimal punctuation.

> chexmix: u get what i asked?
> fruitloop: *in mint condition*
> chexmix: when can u deliver
> fruitloop: *10 tonite at parking lot. bring $*
> chexmix: c ya there

[15.8.3] One side of overheard phone conversation

In the examples below, ellipses show the overheard speaker pausing to listen to the response, which is not heard by the eavesdropper.

In the second example, we put the ellipses in square brackets [...] to denote the other side of the unheard conversation. The third example gives a different rendering, using dashes and conventional ellipses, along with the bracketed ones, to differentiate between the unheard conversation and the first speaker trailing off or being interrupted. You, the writer, should decide which works best for you.

> "Dr. Keller isn't available. May I help you?... I see. I'm sorry to disappoint you, but we have nothing like that in our collection.... No, Dr. Keller is out of the country and I have no idea when he'll be back.... He is traveling. I have no way to contact him at the moment.... No, he does not have a cell phone, but I can take your number and give him the message.... That's the best I can do."

"Dr. Keller isn't available. May I help you? [...] I see. I'm sorry to disappoint you, but we have nothing like that in our collection. [...] No, Dr. Keller is out of the country and I have no idea when he'll be back. [...] He is traveling. I have no way to contact him at the moment. [...] No, he does not have a cell phone, but I can take your number and give him the message. [...] That's the best I can do."

"Dr. Keller isn't available. May I help—? [...] I see. I'm sorry but we have... nothing like that in our collection. [...] No, Dr. Keller is out of the country— [...] I have no— [...] —no idea when he'll be back. He is... traveling. I have no way to contact him at the moment. [...] No, he does not have a cell phone, but I can take your number and give him the message. [...] That's the best I can do."

[15.8.4] Telepathic conversations and projected thoughts

If your characters communicate telepathically some of the time, you may wish to differentiate projected and telepathic communication from internal direct thoughts. One way is to italicize the projected thoughts *and* put them in quotes. This treats telepathic thoughts as an extension of normal dialogue.

You could use special dialogue tags to distinguish such thoughts, but you risk those getting annoying if done too much. The technique you choose for a particular story will depend on the frequency of mental conversations. If the projected thoughts (in italics and with quotation marks) are interspersed with non-projected thoughts (italics, no quotes), the reader might find it difficult to keep them straight. The example below uses this technique.

=====

He whispered in my ear, "I can distract him while you get the artifact."

I shook my head, hoping he saw me. Even if I could grab it, I'd only have a few seconds to figure out how to tap into its power because the bad guy didn't need it to blow me apart. I turned my eyes skyward and wondered, *If I miraculously succeed in this, will they put an ugly statue of me in the Galactic Hall of Fame?*

Thoughts boomed again in my brain, *"WHEN THE SUN SETS HERE AGAIN, I WILL BEGIN MY CONQUEST."*

Another team member—I wasn't sure whose side he was on—stood next to our enemy and pointed down to where Jake was hiding. *"Others came with me. They hide below and believe I'm on their side against you. Show them your power."* Half of what remained of the already crumbling amphitheater blew up. *Jake? Is he okay?*

=====

Although it's easy enough to distinguish the dialogue from the thoughts in italics, the passage also contains internal thoughts. (2nd and 4th paragraphs, and these are differentiated only by the quote marks). Also, two different characters are projecting thoughts here (3rd and 4th paragraphs). We put those of the more powerful character (booming thoughts) in all caps.

ALL CAPS is an option for projected thoughts if they are occasional, but it is distracting otherwise.

You could treat telepathic conversations like normal dialogue and use tags to differentiate them.

Other techniques include enclosing the projected thoughts with slash marks, brackets, or braces. Avoid using asterisks or equal signs as those have other meanings in text formatting. This is where the writer can be a bit creative, but use good judgment as well. Here's an example using slash marks and italics to show the projected thoughts. Regular direct thoughts are just italicized.

=====

Thoughts boomed again in my brain, */WHEN THE SUN SETS HERE AGAIN, I WILL BEGIN MY CONQUEST./*
Another team member—I wasn't sure whose side he was on—stood next to our enemy and pointed down to where Jake was hiding. */Others came with me. They hide below and believe I'm on their side against you. Show them your power./* Half of what remained of the already crumbling amphitheater blew up. *Jake? Is he okay?*

=====

[15.8.5] Sign Language

If characters are employing sign language, one obvious way to render it is by enclosing the translation in quotation marks and employing an appropriate tag. One can also use italics, either in quotes or not. The following passage uses all three options for illustration, but you would use only one of these methods.

=====

Careful not to give away their position to the enemy, Jared signed, "How many are there?" (quotes with tag)

Rand signed back, *Four of them approaching from the east.*" (quotes, italics, with tag)

Jared shifted his night-vision scope in that direction, then signed to his partner, *Got them.* (italics with tag)

=====

This works fine when the conversation is all sign language. If the dialogue includes verbal responses, direct thoughts, and perhaps telepathic projections, you need other methods.

Some foreign languages use guillemets (« ») instead of quotation marks to enclose dialogue. Here's the previous passage revised to include speech, sign language, and thoughts, all clearly differentiated and using guillemets for the sign language.

=====

Careful not to speak and maybe give away their position to the enemy, Jared signed to his partner, «How many are there?»

«Four of them approaching from the east,» Rand replied.

Jared shifted his night-vision scope in that direction. *I wish I had Rand's darksight.* "Got them," he whispered.

=====

NOTE: Guillemets (pronounced in English as *gee-MET* or *gee-MAY*, with a hard "g" as in "geese" and the "s" silent) are analogous to the double quotation mark.

In Windows, you enter guillemets with ALT 0171 and ALT 0187.

On a Mac, use OPTION-BACKSLASH and OPTION-SHIFT-BACKSLASH respectively. The backslash is the "\" key.

These are by no means the only options. One can consider enclosing the sign language in some other set of symbols, as we suggested for telepathic thoughts, as long as the reader understands your intent.

CHAPTER SIXTEEN

SPECIAL TOPICS

[16.1] Accented letters in foreign languages

All letters and symbols have a key code. In MS Word, the INSERT/Symbols menu is one method of entering these symbols. You can enter them with keycodes.

We've compiled a list of the ALT CODES for the accented letters you're mostly likely to use. (Refer to [INTRO.3.1] on how to enter these.)

À	Alt 0192	à	Alt 0224
Á	Alt 0193	á	Alt 0225
Â	Alt 0194	â	Alt 0226
Ä	Alt 0196	ä	Alt 0228
Ç	Alt 0199	ç	Alt 0231
È	Alt 0200	è	Alt 0232
É	Alt 0201	é	Alt 0233
Ê	Alt 0202	ê	Alt 0234
Ë	Alt 0203	ë	Alt 0235
Ì	Alt 0204	ì	Alt 0236
Í	Alt 0205	í	Alt 0237
Î	Alt 0206	î	Alt 0238
Ï	Alt 0207	ï	Alt 0239
Ñ	Alt 0209	ñ	Alt 0241
Ò	Alt 0210	ò	Alt 0242
Ó	Alt 0211	ó	Alt 0243
Ô	Alt 0212	ô	Alt 0244
Ö	Alt 0214	ö	Alt 0246
Ù	Alt 0217	ù	Alt 0249
Ú	Alt 0218	ú	Alt 0250
Ü	Alt 0220	ü	Alt 0252
Û	Alt 0219	û	Alt 0251

[16.2] The slash

The slash (/) is also called a forward slash to differentiate it from the backward slash (\). Normally you do not put spaces before or after the slash. (But see 16.2.4] for one exception.

[16.2.1] Slash to indicate alternatives

The slash can signify alternatives, alternative spellings, or alternative names:

he/she, his/her, and/or, Jupiter/Zeus

It can mean "and" in certain situations:

She is an MD/PhD and a very smart lady.

He has a Jekyll/Hyde personality.

NOTE: Despite being in common use, the familiar "and/or" is often ambiguous in its meaning and should be avoided by good writers. (See[16.2.5])

[16.2.2] Slash in dates or two-year spans

1991/92

12/25/96

[16.2.3] Slash for "per" or "divided by"

$25/hour

52/13=4

[16.2.4] Slash to separate lines of poetry

The slash is used to show separate lines of poetry when they are quoted with other text. When used this way, the slash is separated by a space on each side of it.

I think that I shall never see / A poem as lovely as a tree.

[16.2.5] Improper slash for alternatives

We hear "and/or" used a lot in our speech, but this is ambiguous and poor usage in writing.

[AWKWARD] We can rent a movie and/or play a video game.

This means both "We can rent a movie *and* play a video game" and "We can rent a movie *or* play a video game" at the same time, which is rather awkward. Such use of the slash is lazy writing. We've tried to teach you how to use punctuation to express yourself precisely and clearly.

[BETTER] We can rent a movie or play a video or do both.

[AWKWARD] I want a piece of cake and/or pie. (Do you want cake or pie or both? Don't let someone else decide. Specify what you want.)

[AWKWARD] "He has a large binder/notebook." (Is it a binder, or a notebook? They're not the same thing.)

[16.3] Other marks & symbols for special needs

Be careful when using other symbols for special needs. Some symbols may not render properly in e-books and could show up as something strange (often as a small square box).

Do *not* use the angle brackets (above the period comma and period on the keyboard) for formatting. Those are reserved for enclosing HTML codes and could yield unexpected results in an e-book.

[16.4] Footnotes & asides in fiction

We have seen some authors use actual footnotes at the bottom of pages in fiction. Be aware that these cause the reader to shift attention from the narrative to the bottom of the page and will thus distract from the reading.

True footnotes are only viable in print books or in e-books with a fixed page format. In e-books with reflowable text, the footnote text could fall in the middle of a page, something you want to avoid.

Putting notes in parentheses (or in square brackets, which will set them off better than parentheses) may be a good choice, but be aware that they can also distract from the narrative.

Alternatively, a numbered note in brackets can refer the reader to the note in an appendix.

We feel that fiction should, in general, not use footnotes. A better option is to avoid the necessity for such explanatory notes. Writers should attempt to integrate the information smoothly into the narrative.

[16.5] Inventive uses of punctuation marks

[16.5.1] Solo question marks on a blank line

A rare use of the question mark, especially in lighter writing, has two or three question marks on a separate line to indicate a character's confusion as an indirect thought.

=====

Ryan listened through the crack in the door to Eric and Jacob's conversation.

"So, who gets to do it?" Jacob asked.

Eric shrugged. "Well, I'm sure not going to do it. Are you volunteering?"

"No, but Ryan is our friend."

???

"Yeah, well, he's not here, and someone's gotta do it."

=====

[16.5.2] The colon to assist with a story transition

You might use a colon with a word or phrase on a line by itself to create a transition.

=====

You're a writer. You probably have an alter ego, someone who is a bit larger than you are, more expansive. More daring? He may or may not have appeared in your fiction somewhere. Maybe more than once?

So:

I have this friend who's also a writer. That's "friend," and just so there's no confusion, she's a female, non-male. I know this will sound corny, but her alter ego didn't stay on paper. Her name is Kelly; mine is, well, it's Alek.

=====

This use of the colon might make some purists cringe, but one purpose of the colon is to pull the reader forward, and this one does that—somewhat unconventionally—to serve the voice of the piece, which is one purpose of punctuation.

[16.6] Creative punctuation for made-up words

Sci-fi and fantasy writers sometimes (often?) need to make up words. This is fine, but we advise common sense. Avoid apostrophes in words and character names. While a seemingly harmless way of adding an otherworldly touch, we've heard enough complaints about apostrophes in names over the years to advise against it.

Readers, used to the apostrophe for possessives and contractions, don't always know what to make of them in unexpected places. Made-up and unpronounceable words that confuse a reader have the same effect as misusing punctuation.

"I am Najat`aqvesh Wot' Anuhyam`ak. You may call me Naj," the dragon said.

Whoa! We used two different types of apostrophes. Does that backwards quote-like mark affect the pronunciation? Consider a more reader-friendly approach:

"I am Najat-aqvesh Anuyam. You may call me Naj," the dragon said.

NOTE: That back quote mark used in the first example is also called a *grave* accent (the *a* is pronounced either like in *ray* or in *father*). You see it above some letters in foreign languages. (See [16.1]) We also see it in some poetry and in song lyrics to stress the "*ed*" at the end of some verbs by adding an extra syllable where the *e* is otherwise silent. In the past, the grave accent was used to distinguish *learned* (the past tense of *learn*) from the adjective *learned* (educated) where the "*ed*" is pronounced. Its use is optional: "He is a learned/learnèd man."

[16.7] Special capitalization rules

Sometimes a writer is confused as to whether to capitalize words referring to titles of office (mayor, president, sheriff, colonel, general, senator). One does *not* capitalize these unless the title is used with the person's name, you are addressing the person by title, or the title is substituting for the person's name. When "the" appears in front of the title, do not capitalize it.

Welcome to my home, Senator. (General, Colonel, Mayor, Sheriff)

Our mayor, Stewart Hanrahan, is the youngest our city has ever had.

We were surprised to see Mayor Hanrahan at the dinner party.

The vice-chairman will address the general assembly tomorrow because Chairman Keating is out of town on business.

Walter Diamond, as president of the university, will be at the groundbreaking ceremony.

Walter Diamond, University President, will be at the ceremony tomorrow.

However, an "ego rule" can be invoked (in reality as well as fiction) where the person prefers to be capitalized when being referred to. This gives us some flexibility as writers.

The General demanded that all of his staff account for their whereabouts yesterday.

She insisted that she be referred to as the Colonel's Wife instead of Mrs. Collins—I beg the Colonel's Wife's pardon—as if she were royalty.

His honor the Mayor summoned his Chief of Police to his office.

Fiction writers sometimes make up new words that would be proper nouns if they existed in English, or they may be English words used in the context of a proper noun: Assembly Hall, High Lord. The writer determines whether such words should be capitalized. Don't abuse this technique and don't use it purely to emphasize something.

We normally don't capitalize words like *university, council, guild,* and *town,* but you may do so when they hold special importance and represent the shortened form of a proper title.

The Guild promptly dealt with any outside competition in the town. (referring to the Thieves' Guild)

The Council doubled the import tax last month. (referring to the Ruling Council of the town of Branwell)

In a fantasy setting, various creatures (e.g., elves, dwarves, and dragons) would not be capitalized, just as *dog* and *cat* are not normally capitalized, but if these represent a race of creatures (as we do with *Man*), then they can be capitalized.

[16.8] Punctuating a question within another sentence

Sometimes a direct question is part of another sentence, not in dialogue or as a quote within the sentence. The CMOS says that if the question is long or has internal punctuation, you may capitalize it. If the sentence seems awkward, recast it as a direct thought [14.3.6], as an indirect question [4.2.2], or with different punctuation.

Allen looked around at the devastation and asked himself, what did this?

Allen looked around at the devastation. *What did this?*

Allen looked around at the devastation and wondered what had done this.

My only question was, how can I help him when he doesn't want my help? (optional cap on "how")

My only question was how I could help him when he didn't want my help.

Kristin could see the question on all their faces, How are we going to come up with five thousand dollars, in cash, in only three days?

Kristin could see the question on all their faces: How are we going to come up with five thousand dollars, in cash, in only three days?

[16.9] How to choose from punctuation options

We hope that we've given you enough information and examples throughout this book to help you decide what punctuation to use in most situations. When multiple options present themselves, the choice usually lies in the type of emphasis desired, which part of the sentence you want to emphasize, where the sentence falls in the narrative, and what the punctuation is used around it. We know those sound vague, but each situation is different. Review your options. Sometimes it's simply a matter of personal preference.

The colon, the em-dash, and parentheses can all be used to highlight additional information, but each does so in a different way and for different reasons. The colon usually indicates that a list, description, definition, or explanation follows and leads to reader forward.

The em-dash and parentheses may interrupt the sentence to provide additional information, whereas the colon provides a smoother transition to that information. The dash is a forceful interruption; parentheses offer a more polite one.

Enclosing the information in parentheses treats it more as a helpful comment, an aside, or an afterthought. Putting commas around a parenthetical is the least intrusive means, but commas also provide a weaker separation, which may or may not be preferable.

Consider the following example and some variants of it. Although all say the same thing, the mood each conveys is different.

David's next step was clear. He had to find and stop Graeme before the next full moon changed his foe into a werewolf.

David's next step was clear. He had to find and stop Graeme, before the next full moon changed his foe into a werewolf.

David's next step was clear. He had to find and stop Graeme— before the next full moon changed his foe into a werewolf.

David's next step was clear. He had to find and stop Graeme (hopefully before the next full moon changed his foe into a werewolf).

David's next step was clear: find and stop Graeme—before the next full moon changed his foe into a werewolf.

David's next step was clear: find and stop Graeme (if he was lucky) before the next full moon changed his foe into a werewolf.

David's next step—find and stop Graeme before the next full moon changed his foe into a werewolf—was clear.

David's next step was clear. He had to find—and stop—Graeme before the next full moon changed his foe into a werewolf.

David's next step was clear. He had to find (and stop if possible) Graeme before the next full moon changed his foe into a werewolf.

Let's look at one more variant. In the same way that we tested for incorrect commas in [5.31], we can test dashes. If you can delete the material set off with the dash (or dashes) and still have the sentence make sense, then the dashes are placed correctly.

[INCORRECT] David's next step—find and stop—Graeme before the next full moon.

This fails our test: "David's next step Graeme before the next full moon" is nonsensical.

[CORRECT] David's next step—to find and stop Graeme before the next full moon—depended more on luck than his determination.

Here's another example.

Our party consisted of two factions: those who knew some or all of what was going on—Kedda and Jake—and those who didn't—Jen-Varth, Trax, Enelle, me.

The dashes are correctly used, but the hyphenated name (Jen-Varth) after a dash confuses the eye.

[REVISED] Our party consisted of two factions: those who knew some or all of what was going on (Kedda and Jake), and those who didn't (Jen-Varth, Trax, Enelle, and me).

Consider this example:

If I didn't give it a shot, I'd always wonder what if?

How should the "what if" be punctuated? The choice depends on whether the character is saying it to someone or we're in the character's head (and if it's a direct or an indirect thought). We'd treat it differently if it closed a scene than if it came in the middle of a scene.

If I didn't give it a shot, I'd always wonder, what if? [comma for slight emphasis]

If I didn't give it a shot, I'd always wonder, "what if?" [more emphasis]

"If I don't give it a shot, I'll always wonder, 'what if?'" [as dialogue]

If I didn't give it a shot, I'd always wonder: what if? [strong emphasis]

If I didn't give it a shot, I'd always wonder, *what if*? [indirect thought plus direct thought]

If I don't give it a shot, I'll always wonder, "what if?" [all a direct thought]

If I don't give it a shot, I'll always wonder: WHAT IF? [all direct thought plus caps for a strong emphasis in a scene ending]

Punctuation isn't always about the conventions but about the flow, rhythm, and tone. How the eye parses the sentence is important. How are the sentences around it punctuated? Should the sentence blend with those around it or stand out?

Use a consistent punctuation style throughout a given piece. Don't use parentheses in one place for a parenthetical if you haven't used them elsewhere for parentheticals. Use the serial comma (or not) consistently.

[16.10] What to do when no rule exists

At several places in this book we've proposed solutions when the style guides are silent, and we've stretched more than a few existing rules. We've tried to build upon existing conventions instead of making up new rules. People have been making up rules for a very long time (as did the Masoretes, who we talked about in Chapter 1). That's how the conventions we have today came into existence. A writer's job is to express his thoughts to his readers. If that means flexing the rules, then do so.

FINAL TIP: Don't be different or clever because you can, but because it serves your story.

ABOUT THE AUTHORS

Rick Taubold

Rick Taubold holds degrees in BS chemistry and biology (University of Akron) and MS and PhD degrees in nutritional biochemistry (University of Illinois). He serves on the Board of Directors of Silver Pen Writers' Association and he co-hosts, with Scott Gamboe, a weekly blog "Write Well, Write to Sell." Rick and his wife publish *Fabula Argentea* magazine, a quarterly online magazine of fiction and live in Rochester, NY. Rick has three traditionally published novels.

www.silverpen.org

www.writewell.silverpen.org

www.fabulaargentea.com

www.ricktaubold.com

Published Books:

More Than Magick (2004, 2009, reissued 2014)

Vampires, Inc. (2009, out of print, under revision)

Vampires Anonymous (2010, out of print, under revision)

Scott Gamboe

Scott was born in Peoria, IL and lived there until he joined the Army at the age of 18. He spent four years as a paratrooper in the 82nd Airborne Division, where he participated in the Panama Invasion and the First Gulf War. In 1995, he earned his Bachelor of Arts degree from the University of Illinois. In 1998, he became a police officer, working in patrol and the Crime Scene Unit before earning a spot on a federal computer crimes task force.

He has published eight novels: three published traditionally, and others self-published as e-books. He lives in Central Illinois with his wife, Jill, and his daughter, Erica.

www.scottgamboe.net

Published books:

The Killing Frost, 2006

The Piaras Legacy, 2008

New Dawn Rising, 2009

Martyr's Inferno, 2011

Archon's Gate, 2011

14 Days 'Til Dawn, 2012

A Matter of Faith, 2012

The Pythagoras Enigma, 2013

Made in the USA
Lexington, KY
22 October 2016